A
Grain
of
Poetry

Also by Herbert Kohl

The Plain Truth of Things (with Colin Greer)

A Call to Character (with Colin Greer)

The Discipline of Hope

The Age of Complexity

36 Children

The Open Classroom

Reading How To

Golden Boy as Anthony Cool:
A Photo Essay on Names and Graffiti

Half the House

View from the Oak (with Judith Kohl)

Growing with Your Children

A Book of Puzzlements

Basic Skills

Growing Minds: On Becoming a Teacher

Mathematical Puzzlements

Making Theater: Developing Plays with Young People

The Question Is College

From Archetype to Zeitgeist:
An Essential Guide to Powerful Ideas

I Won't Learn from You

Should We Burn Babar?

A Grain of Poetry

HOW TO READ
CONTEMPORARY POEMS
AND MAKE THEM A PART
OF YOUR LIFE

Herbert Kohl

Perennial

An Imprint of HarperCollins*Publishers*

A hardcover edition of this book was published in 1999 by Harper-Flamingo, an imprint of HaperCollins Publishers.

HarperCollins books may be purchased for educational, business, or sales promotional use. For information please write: Special Markets Department, HarperCollins Publishers Inc., 10 East 53rd Street, New York, NY 10022.

First Perennial edition published 2000.

Designed by John D. Sparks

The Library of Congress has catalogued the hardcover edition as follows:
Kohl, Herbert R.
    A grain of poetry : how to read contemporary poems and make them part of your life / Herbert Kohl. — 1st ed.
        p. cm.
    ISBN 0-06-018783-2
    1. Poetry—Explication. 2. Poetry, Modern—20th century—History and criticism. I. Title. II. Series.
PN1075.K65 1998
808.1—dc21   98–51444

ISBN 0-06-093071-3 (pbk.)

00 01 02 03 04 ❖/RRD 10 9 8 7 6 5 4 3 2 1

Dedicated to Denise Levertov
whose life and work have been an inspiration

A grain of poetry
suffices to season
a century.

José Martí, *Dedication of*
the Statue of Liberty, 1887

Contents

Acknowledgments   xiii

Introduction   1

Chapter One:
Encountering Poems   21

Chapter Two:
It's the Breaks   41

Chapter Three:
Rhythm and Melody: An Ear for Poetry   67

Chapter Four:
The Images at the Heart of Poems   89

Chapter Five:
The Voice of the Turtle   117

Chapter Six:
The Poet's Eye/The Reader's Eye:
Practicing Reading Poetry   139

Appendix: Reaching Out and Digging In   161

Permissions   169

Acknowledgments

The idea for this book emerged from a lunch conversation I had with Hugh Van Dusen, my editor at HarperCollins. We were talking about the importance of poetry in our lives and the idea of a book about reading poetry emerged. From that day to publication Hugh has been supportive, helpful, and a delight. He loves poetry as much as I do and I hope the energy he put into the making of this book is paid back by the final work.

I also want to thank my wife Judy and my daughter Antonia who have read the manuscript, found poems to include, and dealt with the difficult and often thankless task of arranging for permissions.

In addition thanks are due to Laurie, Armand, Stevie, and Tony Ritchie, and Lorraine Ruddick and David Kelley for their help on the manuscript.

I also want to acknowledge Ashley Crout who has read the manuscript and provided wonderful feedback and research support, as well as given me a sense that the book might have some value for young poets as well as readers of poetry.

Finally, I would like to thank all the poets whose work has inspired me and enhanced my own thinking and writing.

Introduction

Ink runs from the corners
of my mouth.

—Mark Strand

My love of poetry goes back to early adolescence. It had nothing to do with what I learned in school but rather was shaped by wandering among used-book stores on Fourth Avenue in New York City in 1950 and '51. There were few books in my home, and none of them (other than the prayer books written in Hebrew, a language I could recite but not understand) was poetry. School was indifferent on poetry—a few poems were thrown in now and then as manifestations of "culture" but none of them spoke to my turmoil, hopes, dreams, or sense of humor. I remember my father telling me, when I brought home the first book of poetry I bought with my own money, that he remembered a line of poetry from his days in school: "In Stygian caves forlorn." He said he had never forgotten the line and yet didn't have the slightest idea of what it meant. But forlorn he knew and the kind of caves you live in when you are poor or afraid he also knew. The line stayed with him because of the caves and the forlorn, he told me, but from Stygian he knew nothing. He couldn't remember another thing about the poem, neither its author nor its subject. But the memory of a line of verse that stays with one—for him then over seventy years—is part of the argument for poetry.

The first books of poetry I bought were two small volumes of poems published by Castle Books and the Creative Bookmaking

Guild. One was the collected poems of John Keats and the other *The Sonnets of Shakespeare*. They cost 25 cents each and were small enough to fit in my pants pocket so I could carry them around without anyone else in school or on the block knowing that I was reading poetry. They were recommended to me by one of the older men who owned those used-book stores on Fourth Avenue who used to talk about books rather than try to sell them. He said poetry was for me and since I had nothing to lose I tried it and became hooked.

I used to read poems at lunch in junior high school and on the bus on the way to school in my first year of high school. I didn't know anything about Keats or Shakespeare, had never read any literary criticism or known about their stature as a poets. Keats in particular wasn't big in the working-class community in the Bronx that I grew up in. But he was for me—spoke to a world beyond my own world in images and phrases that both moved me and made me aware of the imaginative possibilities of language. Besides, Keats spoke of voyaging, of adventure and exploration. I wanted to stand "Silent, upon a peak in Darien," though I didn't even know where Darien was, much less dream of the sight of the Pacific. Several lines from one of Keats's sonnets I encountered in that book or maybe later when I read more extensively in his work has stayed with me like my father's Stygian caves:

> To one who has been long in city pent,
> 'Tis very sweet to look into the fair
> And open face of heaven.

I knew as an adolescent what it meant to be pent up and was sure that I had been long in a city pent and needed to get out. It's ironic to me, thinking back on those lines, that now I live on eleven acres in northern California and can see myself dreaming of this very place when I was twelve in the Bronx, living in the shadow of the Lexington Avenue El and bombarded by the sounds of the comings and goings of the trains. I had never seen the "open face of heaven," but could imagine it from the poem.

There are times these days I miss that freshness of encountering a poem without any mediating judgments, and reading contemporary poems often brings me back to that innocence and clarity. It's wonderful to discover and read a poem when you know nothing about the poet, have never read critical commentary on the work, and have to figure out what the poet is doing with language. Sometimes there are wonderful revelations, at other times confusion or boredom. Not every poem speaks to me, nor is every poem that moves me extraordinary. There are poems that move other people that leave me cold, and poets with major reputations whose work I don't enjoy even though I know it is well written and moves other people. That is part of the magic of reading around in poetry—some of it will move you, some will move your friends, and some will simply be put aside. Reading poetry for yourself does not imply making critical judgments. It does, however require knowing a bit about how to read modern poems, and how to be patient and give yourself to the language and sentiments of a poem. It is easy to learn how to do this and important as an antidote to media babble and the confusion of information with understanding. Modern poetry is as useful in making sense out of our complex reality as the best of newspapers and journals, and is more personal. This book is about just reading poetry and letting it speak to you. It is for the reader of poems, not the critic or historian of poetry. It is not going to provide a guide to what is good and bad poetry. If anything, it is an attempt to educate your judgment as a reader of poems and let you decide for yourself what you like, what you love, what you find boring or inaccessible, or what does not move you at all. Intelligent readership depends upon the informed judgments and tastes of the reader, not fashion, critical approval, or what others think. Taste in poetry, as in other personal things, is an internal matter, an examination of self as much as a reaching out to the voices of others. If this book can do anything useful, it would be to help you listen to the voices, insights, imaginations, and language of poets writing now, and to give you the confidence to make your own judgments about the poems and poets you find of value.

Contemporary poems speak in a particular way that distinguishes them from newspapers, novels, and conversation with friends. They speak in a multiplicity of voices and often with freedom from the usual conventions of grammar, spelling, and syntax. Sometimes we need to listen to people talking at the edges of language. Poetry speaks more intimately, wildly, and provocatively than the manners of ordinary conversation allow. The rules of rhyme, meter, and stanza, though often respected by poets writing now, are just a small part of their repertory. The far margins of grammar and intimacy, the possibility of painting words on a page with letters being brush strokes, and the challenge of making language alive and truthful in the face of media sham intrigues poets. And for many of them the expression of self and culture intersect and illuminate the complex interaction of heritage and aspiration. Poetry is a form of song, a boundary art between music and conversation.

The poet Denise Levertov speaks, in her poem "The Secret," of the power of poetry to transform lives, and of the complex dialogue between poet and reader:

Two girls discover
the secret of life
in a sudden line of
poetry.

I who don't know the
secret wrote
the line. They
told me

(through a third person)
they had found it
but not what it was
not even

what line it was. No doubt
by now, more than a week
later, they have forgotten
the secret,

the line, the name of
the poem. I love them
for finding what
I can't find,

and for loving me
for the line I wrote,
and for forgetting it
so that

a thousand times, till death
finds them, they may
discover it again, in other
lines

in other
happenings. And for
wanting to know it,
for

assuming there is
such a secret, yes
for that
most of all.

The intent of the poet does not just reside in being admired. Levertov is not looking for praise for her skill. It is more important to move readers than to have them as approving critics—to have them feel wonder about the quest for the elusive secret of life rather than admiration for her poetic techniques. But the poem itself has a form that makes the reading of it accessible. The last line of each stanza is short and it leads on to the next verse. The first stanza is a complete statement but after that each one ends in a phrase that leads you on: "told me," "not even," "the secret," "I can't find," "so that," "lines," "for," and at the very end, "most of all." Each line has been crafted to introduce a thought and the next two lines chosen to complete it. The poem creates a dialogue with the reader. It is a skillfully edited meditation about hope in which Denise, her young readers, and current readers are all engaged. There is no word in the poem that could not be read by a third grader and yet the content can move at any age.

Poetry begs contemplation and time and involves continual acts of discovery. As Levertov says, she hopes these young readers, and by implication all of her readers, will discover such secrets "in other/lines"—that where they found revelation in one poem they can also find it in other poetry.

She hopes, as most poets do, that their poems are not the only ones, that their verses are not the only ones. Poetry is not a contest, though poetry slams, where poets compete against each other in front of live audiences, as well as other competitions, can be fun or motivating for poets. Poetry has as the sources of its inspiration the personal experience of poets, the demands and complexities of the historical moment in which the poem is written, and the challenging brilliance and experimentation with language of the poets who have come before. Read this short poem by William Carlos Williams, "The Red Wheelbarrow" out loud several times and in different tones. Pay special attention to how you read the first two lines:

so much depends
upon

a red wheel
barrow

glazed with rain
water

beside the white
chickens

What is it that might depend upon this red wheelbarrow and why is this considered an important poem or even a poem at all? It could have been a line from a murder story in an newspaper about the crime scene if scanned this way:

> so much depends upon a red wheelbarrow glazed with rain
> water beside the white chickens

What makes it a poem and what makes the poet write this way? Think of it this way: Maybe you fall in love with a cat you see on your way to work every day and worry about it when it rains. Or maybe you see the same homeless person day after day and wonder about what she thinks and feels. Or maybe in the country you see a red wheelbarrow on someone's lawn, glazed with rain water, with chickens running around it and you wonder why it was there, who wheeled it, what was its necessary function in the lives of people in this unknown place, and how their lives depended on being able to carry things they could not lift up.

This simple poem, as particular and direct as its central image is, also raises big questions in a concrete and immediate way. The red wheelbarrow is qualified by the first lines: "so much depends/upon." Before we even read about the object, we have to be sensitive to its importance. But because it is ordinary, the quality of ordinary objects and by implication the everyday ordinary things of our lives are set in the context of our larger worlds. "So much" are the important words here. The poem does not say "something depends upon," or "it depends upon," or even "everything depends upon." "So much" is a challenge—how much is that, what do objects say of our lives, how can we make sense of the daily round? A short and simple poem can raise difficult and complex questions.

William Carlos Williams's poem does not tell anyone what or how to think but teases thoughts and associations out of a concrete image. This movement from the concrete to the abstract and the emotional is just one of the powers of modern poetry. And the form Williams chooses to shape this poem is not arbitrary.

His editor, James Laughlin, at New Directions Books, in a memoir
of his relationship with Williams, indicates how conscious the poet
was about shaping his poem. The following selection, written in a
style similar to Williams's, gives an indication of how modern
poets expanded the ways in which words can appear on a page and
reading could become expanded to become closer to spoken and
inflected language. It refers to Williams' masterpiece, "Paterson":

> For *Paterson* he
> Wanted something far more
> Visual and expressive. Broken
> Lines, short lines mixed with
> Long lines, variations in
> Vertical spacing, in short
> A page where the type would
> Float free, as unrestrained as
> The ideas the words were stating.
> He wanted to liberate the words
> And lines on the page. Bill had
> A strong visual sense. As a young
> Man he had done some creditable
> Painting. From the days of the
> Armory Show of 1913 he had been
> Interested in painting and had
> Close painter friends. From his
> Trips to Europe he knew what
> Apollinaire had done with his
> *Calligrammes* and how the Dadaists
> And Surrealists had experimented
> With typography. It was only
> Natural that he should conceive
> Of a page of type as a free-form
> Design. When I showed Bill's
> Script to our salesman at Haddon
> Craftsmen, the commercial printer
> New Directions often used, he
> Said that such composition

Would cost an arm and a leg;
The irregular spacing couldn't
Be done by linotype. By luck I
Had heard of a small printer,
George W. Van Vechten in
Metuchen, New Jersey, who
Enjoyed solving typographical
Problems in books.

Sometimes the central image in a poem holds together joy, love, and unbearable pain and the shape of the poem is chosen to build up an emotional rhythm that cannot be conveyed by simply telling the reader in prose what one is thinking or feeling. In "She Had Some Horses" Joy Harjo chooses horses as her central image or metaphor. The poem is part autobiography, part scream, part affirmation. The horses provide the visual images that frame the words and content. This could have been an essay on Joy Harjo's experiences. But the image of horses provides motion–galloping, wild energy. Joy Harjo speaks from her experience as a Native American, but the poem also makes sense to many people who are not Native Americans. Her words, at least for me, tell as much about people I know and live with as they do about her and her world. It never makes sense to look at a poem as ethnic, feminist, and so on, or to put it in any category. Take it into yourself and learn whether it speaks to you from its particular perspective to the things you share with the poet as a lively, imaginative, and sensitive person:

She Had Some Horses

She had some horses.

She had horses who were bodies of sand.
She had horses who were maps drawn of blood.
She had horses who were skins of ocean water.
She had horses who were the blue air of sky.
She had horses who were fur and teeth.

She had horses who were clay and would break.
She had horses who were splintered red cliffs.

She had some horses.

She had horses with long, pointed breasts.
She had horses with full, brown thighs.
She had horses who laughed too much.
She had horses who threw rocks at glass houses.
She had horses who licked razor blades.

She had some horses.

She had horses who danced in their mothers' arms.
She had horses who thought they were the sun and their
    bodies shone and burned like stars.
She had horses who waltzed nightly on the moon.
She had horses who were much too shy, and kept quiet
    in stalls of their own making.

She had some horses.
She had horses who liked Creek Stomp Dance songs.
She had horses who cried in their beer.
She had horses who spit at male queens who made
    them afraid of themselves.
She had horses who said they weren't afraid.
She had horses who lied.
She had horses who told the truth, who were stripped
    bare of their tongues.

She had some horses.

She had horses who called themselves, "horse."
She had horses who called themselves, "spirit," and kept
    their voices secret and to themselves.
She had horses who had no names.
She had horses who had books of names.
She had some horses.

She had horses who whispered in the dark, who were
    afraid to speak. She had horses who screamed out
    of fear of the silence, who carried knives to protect
    themselves from ghosts.
She had horses who waited for destruction.
She had horses who waited for resurrection.

She had some horses.

She had horses who got down on their knees for any
    savior.
She had horses who thought their high price had saved
    them.
She had horses who tried to save her, who climbed in her
    bed at night and prayed as they raped her.

She had some horses.

She had some horses she loved.
She had some horses she hated

These were the same horses.

Poetry has the power to move and challenge us. It can confirm
your feeling that life is worth something after all when you are
down, out, and tired. It can also intensify or even celebrate misery,
be cynical or wry, or just laugh outright in an outrageous way.
Poetry is as serious and as antic as life. When you approach a
poem, it's important to know that poets speak in many voices. The
emotional rules of poetry are as open and flexible as the rules of
language, and the emotions expressed in poetry are as complex as
those we feel over a lifetime.

Sometimes poems are like snapshots that capture a moment and at
the same time reveal how connected that particular view is to the larger
movements of life on the planet. Robert Hass, former American Poet
Laureate, expresses that in this short poem that could not be reduced
to an article on bird migrations published in *Scientific American:*

Migration
A small brown wren in the tangle
of the climbing rose. April:
last rain, the first dazzle
and reluctance of the light.

The "reluctance of the light" creates a tension, a sense of the sun's presence as well as intimations of its absence. There is slow movement and process in this poem which, when read quietly several times, becomes a miniature portrait or maybe more precisely a short film, only one that is better rendered by words than photos. The rose climbs too slowly to be seen in a short film; we can imagine the last rain; and the wren infuses the whole with the sense of a temporary visitation. This is a sensual representation of what the title implies: migration, the regular path through seasons and geographies that the Earth and all on it partake of. I find it sweet and moving. It reminds me of Emily Dickinson's quote, "If I read a book and it makes my whole body so cold no fire can ever warm me, I know that is poetry. If I feel physically as if the top of my head were taken off, I know that is poetry. These are the only ways I know it. Is there any other way?" Hass's poem does not make my body cold but it does gently lift the top of my head off and let the exposed brain take in something new and affecting.

We are not all Emily Dickinson, and there are many other ways to know and love poetry. The possibility of such intense response to a poem often distracts people from the other delights and provocations of contemporary poetry. These can be personal, sometimes intimate to the point of embarrassment, but they also can celebrate culture and community. Sometimes they are just plain celebratory or embody rage, love, injury, sadness, wonder, or joy. Poetry is ritual and song, stepping out of the ordinary at times and confronting norms of belief and practice, or celebrating it at others. Poems can fill in the corners of our lives where we are lonely or in search of a new voice, a new image, a new idea. They can confirm our unique importance or be a reminder that we are finite and vulnerable.

And yet reading contemporary poems can be difficult, shocking to our sense of what language is or must be. Expectations of what poetry has to sound like or talk about come from old school memories of rhyme and meter. It is easy to avoid or resist freshness in language because it can be so disorienting. Marianne Moore expresses the problems and promises of contemporary poetry this way:

> I, too, dislike it
> Reading it, however, with a perfect contempt for it, one discovers in
> it, after all, a place for the genuine.

The line "a place for the genuine" implies that authenticity is an uncommon experience. However, it does not imply that modern poetry is grim or overserious or lacking in irony or a sense of play. Genuine writing can be frank and direct, but it can also be indirect, full of double meanings and allusions, and governed by images that cannot easily be translated into ordinary prose. I believe that what Moore meant by "genuine" has more to do with the attempt to wrestle with an experience at the edge of language and to say things that do not easily translate into simple direct sentences.

Here is an encounter with the genuine from Martin Espada:

The Right Hand of a Mexican Farmworker
in Somerset County, Maryland
A rosary tattoo
between thumb
and forefinger
means that
every handful
of crops and dirt
is a prayer,
means that Christ
had hard hands
too

Here is another encounter with the genuine, although it is

manifested in an indirect, delightfully irreverent poem by Peter
Blue Cloud (Aroniawenrate):

> *Frybread Story*
> Coyote was making frybread dough
> when young Magpie stopped in
> to offer his own recipe.
>
> An extra handful of flour and
> another dash of salt, he said,
> would assure very fine results.
>
> Coyote chased him away, shouting,
> "I'm not making fine results,
>   you asshole,
>   I'm making frybread."

And here is very different, more personal one, from Adrienne
Rich:

> *Delta*
> If you have taken this rubble for my past
> raking through it for fragments you could sell
> know that I long ago moved on
> deeper into the heart of the matter
>
> If you think you can grasp me, think again;
> my story flows in more than one direction
> a delta springing from the riverbed
> with its five fingers spread

Even belly buttons, 2,000 of them, can be the stuff of poetry.
Victor Hernández Cruz, in this anti-gravity poem, provides a wide
flight of the imagination that, as Hernández Cruz says in the poem,
"turn / Belly buttons into brushes." Poems can fly, and the habit of
reading poems is sometimes to give oneself up to the language,
rhythm, or the wild flights of imagination of the poet.

Agriculture
It is raining up
Not water
But belly buttons in
The plaza.
I am telling you this—
2,000 I see near
The ceiba tree.
Consequently umbrellas
Should be horizontal mouths
Facing down and wide open
Abandon all function
Give in to the
Pleasures of reversed
Gravity to its dream,
A world between belt
And shirt
Where bellies were tied
Like balloons.
With a strong pull out of
The ground
Where earthworms
Are librarians
Giving it on loan
Guava with fishnet
Stockings—
This is all without
The slightest intention
Of music
Lyrics which will turn
Belly buttons into brushes
Painting circles—
As the insects cross
Into the vibration
Under the flight of
Invisible parrots

Which are parallel
To white dresses
Whose upper embroidery
Is a closed curtain
For dancing guanavanas.

Poems are full of relationships and juxtapositions that tease the imagination and speak to the heart of human experience. Jane Hirshfield could be describing the imaginative workings of the poetic imagination in the next poem, which, also uses the image of a paintbrush, though of course there are many other ways to experience and interpret the poem. There is no single and unambiguous reading of a poem. It depends upon the reader's experience as well as the experience of the poet, and so reading poetry is a form of engaging in dialogue. It is a conversation, not with the poet, but with her or his work, in the same way that listening to music and looking at a painting involve the experience and the creative and critical input of the listener and the viewer. That's part of the pleasure of reading poems. As a reader you are active, not passive.

Lying
He puts his brush to the canvas,
with one quick stroke
unfolds a bird from the sky.
Steps back, considers.
Takes pity,
Unfolds another.

Imagine yourself painting as you read this, and moving your hand as if you were in front of a canvas. Of course, it's not necessary to be that dramatic in order to read a poem well and with power. But relating to poems in a visceral and physical way can often enhance the experience of engaging in poetry. Certainly it helps as you read this selection to imagine a bird emerging from a simple brush stroke. It intensifies the emotions expressed in the line "Takes pity," which raises a question, a puzzlement. Why pity in the bringing forth of a bird? And why move on and bring another painted bird into the world?

Much modern poetry is underground communication expressing intimate and subversive ideas and feelings in ways that encourage multiple readings. Reading poetry is different from reading the newspaper, and letting the meaning of a poem settle in is not the same as learning textbook information. Perhaps it is more like listening to music. Former American Poet Laureate Rita Dove expresses something of this quality in her poem "Canary" dedicated to the poet Michael S. Harper:

> Billie Holiday's burned voice
> had as many shadows as lights,
> a mournful candelabra against a sleek piano,
> the gardenia her signature under that ruined face.
> (Now you're cooking, drummer to bass,
> magic spoon, magic needle.
> Take all day if you have to
> with your mirror and your bracelet of song.)
>
> Fact is, the invention of women under siege
> has been to sharpen love in the service of myth.
>
> If you can't be free, be a mystery.

What all of these poems have in common is the uncommon voices of people speaking from their hearts in condensed and vivid language. That is what modern poetry does: speak out of grammar and time to deeply felt issues, problems, and experiences. The language of poetry moves between meditation, dream, and conversation. It does not tie things up neatly or allow for single interpretations. It thrives on complexity and is based on the freedom that language provides at its margins and boundaries.

Consider for example the first four lines of this poem (translated from the Hebrew) by the Israeli poet Yehuda Amachai:

A Pity. We Were Such a Good Invention
They amputated
Your thighs off my hips.
As far as I'm concerned
They are all surgeons. All of them.

They dismantled us
Each from the other.
As far as I'm concerned
They are all engineers. All of them.

A pity. We were such a good
and loving invention.
An aeroplane made from a man and wife.
Wings and everything.
We hovered a little above the earth.

We even flew a little.

This love poem begins with an amputation—"Your thighs off my hips." When I first read it I felt the pain the poet expressed taking me to the most wonderful times of making love with my wife and to the separations and amputations we've experienced because the demands of work and love don't always coincide. I hate sleeping alone in motel rooms or traveling to so-called important meetings. There are times when we had to separate, Judy to take care of her father, me to be there during my mother's dying. Amputations are part of love but the amputation Amachai talks of in the poem is more frightening.

But there is also a political way to look at the poem. Who are the "they" that is so central to the poem. Lovers get amputated because of war, oppression, racism, homophobia.

Amachai's poem speaks to amputations and lets the reader fill in the specifics. A poem is not a crossword puzzle with one correct answer. In this poem it is up to us to define and imagine the "they."

Good poems do not have single meanings that can be captured and paraphrased in prose. It challenges us to take the words to our hearts and to value not merely the poem but the reading, understanding, and feeling of it. As T. S. Eliot said in his essay on Dante, "Genuine poetry can communicate before it is understood."

What I hope to do in this book is open the doors to communication with poetry—the whole range and variety of contemporary poetic voices. I am not trying to provide a critical analysis of "good" poetry, so much as a series of guideposts to help people read poetry and find the poems that move them. Maybe then some of the readers will feel what the poet Mark Strand expresses:

> Ink runs from the corners of my mouth.
> There is no happiness like mine.
> I have been eating poetry.

The image of eating poetry reminds me of eating in general. One does not eat spaghetti, endives, or ice cream just once. You don't say I've had spaghetti, let's get on to something else. The same is true with poems. They bear, beg, and need rereading. For that reason a number of the poems in this book are examined from different perspectives in different chapters. My hope is that a return to the same poem after reading more poetry and getting a feel for the ways in which poetry can become accessible will enhance appreciation of the poems and draw the reader deeper into poetry itself.

1

Encountering Poems

Islands
O for God's sake
they are connected
underneath

They look at each other
across the glittering sea
some keep a low profile

Some are cliffs
The bathers think
islands are separate like them

Muriel Rukeyser's short poem could be taken as a metaphor for
the subterranean way in which contemporary poems are con-
nected to each other. There are certain underlying commonalities
that separate this poetry from prose. One is the poet's approach to
the blank page. If you look at a book of nonfiction—whether it is a
biography or autobiography, a sociology text, a book of film or the-
ater criticism, or a personal confession or book of psychological

advice–the page is filled up in the same way. There are headings, paragraphs, perhaps quotes surrounded by quotation marks indented in the standard way. One page resembles another page and one book resembles another book from a visual point of view. Sentences begin with a capital letter and end with a period. Commas and semicolons help the reader know where the pauses are. The same is true for almost all of prose fiction. The form of most prose is predictable, and the reader does not have to adapt her or his sense of what to expect on the page from book to book. In fact, the page is there to be turned, not to be studied or viewed the way one might look at a drawing or photo.

It's different with poetry. The blank page is often treated as a canvas for painting as much as a vehicle for sharing print. The placement of a poem on a page, or over several pages, and the shape of the poem create a visual composition as well as a verbal one. That means one has to look as well as read when encountering a poem, and sometimes something as simple as looking at the whole poem and its form before even reading a word can help orient you to the structure the poet has created. I know that when I approach a new poem one of the first things I do it look at its shape before reading it.

The most important thing when coming to poetry is to take this advice of poet and essayist Philip Lopate:

> People too often assume they're at fault if they don't appreciate a poem. I think they should trust their own instincts. When you find a poet whose style you like, read everything he or she has written. It's really not important to like all poetry, but it's important to start to trust your taste in it and enjoy it.

There are some ways to encounter poems that help develop a personal passion for poetry. One has to do with looking at poems as well as reading them. Sometimes the shape of a poem is explicitly related to its meaning. This is true in what is called Concrete Poetry, where the poem is looked upon as a painting with words. Here's an example of a concrete poem by Ian Hamilton Finlay:

> star
> **star**
> star
> star
> star
> star
> star
> star
> star
> star
> star
> **steer**

This poem/poster is a representation of steering by a star. It can be interpreted in many ways: to represent the selection of a special star, to show affinity (through the bold type) between a person and the cosmic world, etc. It can also simply be taken in as a pleasant, interesting way in which letters, shapes, and meaning can come together without having to use too many words.

Concrete poetry is only one small island in the world of contemporary poetry, though with the development of computer graphics the combination and transformations of letters and graphic images is quite common. Concrete poetry has been taken over by the computer graphics world (and especially by advertising) and we are much more accustomed to looking at letters as well as reading them these days. This can help in approaching more complex poems where words, meaning, spacing, typography, and images play central roles and the graphic presentation is meant to enhance these other aspects of the poem.

Just as a note, shaping poems is quite old. Here is a shaped poem written by the Elizabethan poet George Herbert and published in 1633. The altar Herbert refers to in the poem is, as the shape indicates, the poem itself.

The Altar

A broken altar, Lord, thy servant rears,
Made of a heart and cemented with tears;
Whose parts are as thy hand did frame;
No workman's tool hath touched the same.
A heart alone
Is such a stone
As nothing but
Thy power doth cut.
Wherefore each part
Of my hard heart
Meets in this frame
To praise thy name;
That if I chance to hold my peace,
These stones to praise thee may not cease.
Oh, let thy blessed sacrifice be mine
And sanctify this altar to be thine.

Even when the shape of a poem is simple, straightforward, and repetitive, that shape can force a complex reading. The reader is not passive. As the poet, essayist, and novelist Ursula Le Guin has said of reading poem, "You can't just pick up a book of poetry, you have to put some energy into it." Read this poem by Ron Padgett:

Nothing in that drawer.
Nothing in that drawer.
Nothing in that drawer.
Nothing in that drawer.
Nothing in that drawer.
Nothing in that drawer.
Nothing in that drawer.
Nothing in that drawer.

Nothing in that drawer.
Nothing in that drawer.
Nothing in that drawer.
Nothing in that drawer.
Nothing in that drawer.
Nothing in that drawer.

In his marvelous book *Creative Reading*, subtitled *What It Is, How to Do It, and Why*, Padgett raises the following questions about this poem (p. 45): "Did every *nothing* feel the same? Every *in*, *that*, and *drawer*? Is the tone of each line exactly the same as that of every other line? It can't be." Extending Padgett's comments, every reader will render this list in a different way. Some will turn away and say it's boring; others might dramatize it. Some can make it comical, others mysterious or menacing. And some people may simply think it's not worth the energy. The reader's choice, energy, and imagination are always there as part of the reading.

Consider this poem by Robert Creeley. Read it silently for a first time:

I Know a Man
As I sd to my
friend, because I am
always talking,—John, I

sd, which was not his
name, the darkness sur-
rounds us, what

can we do against
it, or else, shall we &
why not, buy a goddamn big car,

drive, he sd, for
christ's sake, look
out where yr going.

On first glimpse it is clear that there are four short stanzas, and the lines are of different lengths. The word "surrounds" is broken at the end of a line, and "and" is replaced by "&." In the first line "said" is written "sd" and there are no quotation marks around the quotes. The whole is resolutely informal and these simple visual clues help the reader to accept the poem on its own terms: not grammatical in the same way that prose is, a bit rambling, full of tricks, breaking all the rules you learned in school, and yet readable and for me fascinating and provocative. Upon first reading it emerges that the poet and his friend are in a car and he is driving and talking, but this is not a linear narrative. It is an anecdote told in a single wandering sentence (there is a capital "A" at the beginning of the poem and a sole period at the end), a small concrete snatch of life that also speaks about something much larger. The poem poses a question about what can be done about the "darkness." And the answer to this question, which is also the answer to the poet's erratic driving and talking, is the simple and powerful stanza:

> drive, he sd, for
> christ's sake, look
> out where yr going.

This poem begs to be reread, read aloud, and for me copied into my book of poems to share with others the way I like to share stories and jokes and anecdotes. The Nobel Prize–winning poet Czeslaw Milosz described poetry in a way that fits Creely's poem:

> Poetry is quite different. By its very nature it says:
> All those theories are untrue. Since poetry deals
> with the singular, not the general, it cannot—if it is
> good poetry—look at things of this earth other than
> as colorful, variegated, and exciting, and so, it cannot
> reduce life, with all its pain, horror, suffering,
> and ecstasy, to a unified tonality of boredom or complaint. By necessity Poetry is therefore on the side of
> being, and against nothingness.

Creely's poem, as informal and easy as it is to read, is highly crafted, a good example of the creative use and breaking of ordinary rules of prose that is characteristic of much of modern poetry. There are wonderful touches—Creely is talking to a friend John, but John is not the friend's name. They are on the road. The poem moves along like the car, erratically, perhaps too fast, on the verge of going out of control. The informal language and the rhythm of the piece, the rolling movement of the poem, get the reader on the road in a particular car at a wild moment and yet confront her or him with a metaphysical question. What fun.

Here's another poem, by Jane Hirshfield, that plays with space and the rules of grammar in less obvious ways. Look at it, skim it before reading, and try to orient yourself to the shape and structure of the poem. Look for regularities and then for ways in which they are broken. The title of the poem provides a hint about the way to read it: "If the Rise of the Fish." Skimming the poem, the "if" structure becomes apparent. Get comfortable with the repetitive structure of the poem and its dependence upon the conditional mode. The "if" sets the poem in the possible, not the actual; it is about possibility and hope. Take your time. Reading a poem is never a one-time thing, and many new readers of poetry think they should get everything at once, or be moved by the poem right away. Much poetry takes a while to sink in. It requires feeling your way into the poem, letting the images sit in your mind, hearing the rhythm of the poetry and the voice of the poet. Music is often the same way. You can come to love a song that didn't move you at all the first time you heard it.

If the Rise of the Fish
If for a moment
the leaves fell upward,
if it seemed a small flock
of brown-orange birds
circled over the trees,
if they circled then scattered each in
its own direction for the lost seed
they had spotted in tall, gold-checkered grass.

If the bloom of flies on the window
in morning sun, if their singing insistence
on grief and desire. If the fish.
If the rise of the fish.
If the blue morning held in the glass of the window,
if my fingers, my palms. If my thighs.
If your hands, if my thighs.
If the seeds, among all the lost gold of the grass.
If your hands on my thighs, if your tongue.
If the leaves. If the singing fell upward. If grief.
For a moment if singing and grief.
If the blue of the body fell upward, out of our hands.
If the morning held it like leaves.

Here the rhythm of the "if"; the incomplete sentences; the repetition of the words "thighs," "grief," "upward," and "hands"; the long and short lines, modifying the way in which the images and voice move; all contribute to the power of the poem. Getting a feel for some of these attributes makes reading easier and lets one turn to the images and the emotional flow of the poem, to its anti-gravity orientation. This allows a reader, on rereading the poem, to be carried along with it and let the first tentative reading of the work become fluent a second or third time around. The energy you put into a poem can often come back in the pleasure and insight it provides when you reach the point where the poem flows like a song.

Of course, some readers will prefer to jump right in and not worry about noticing these elements of the poem. However, attending to the structure of a poem, to its placement on the page, to the way in which grammar is shaped by the poet, all can be useful in approaching a new form and helping the reader become oriented to the writer and her or his poems. This is not a question of criticizing what the poet is doing or making a judgment on the quality of the poem. It is preliminary to judgment, preparation for reading.

"Agriculture" by Victor Hernández Cruz, quoted in the Introduction and beginning:

It is raining up
Not water
But belly buttons in
The plaza.
I am telling you this—
2,000 I see near
The ceiba tree.

also uses anti-gravity as a central image and is wonderful to contrast with Jane Hirshfield's "The Rise of the Fish."

Here is a poem by Juan Delgado that breaks with prose and traditional poetry in a more dramatic way. The title is also the first line of the poem, which happens often in contemporary poems.

When You Leave
Carry pride in your fist,
     walk,
   stop only to check the time,
know the corner store,
      turn and smile back,
   whistling past the barking dog.

Sit at a bar stool,
   never too warm,
      never
   be the first to talk
   of politics or sports.

When listening to a lady
   never rattle
your change, unless
   she's doing you,
doing you the business first,
    Be always willing
   not to lead.

Nod even if you disagree,
                         listen,
               pretending is an art.

Never repeat this,
                    especially to lovers who seek
               your advice on matters.

Wear your eyes in shade,
               rest under dreamy suns,
               and sing if you have to,
               fall in love if you have to,
               but only to the day's motion,
     simply silent and in transition, always.

The visual structure of this poem is clear: stanzas beginning
with single lines starting at the left margin, followed by indented
lines as if the indented lines were comments or annotations. This
makes sense since the poem is about preparations: "When You
Leave," not after you've gone. It is a poem of advice, perhaps to the
poet himself but certainly to someone who is trying to leave the bar-
rio. But as an island that connects to other poems and to other peo-
ple's experiences, it is a metaphor about leaving that could apply to
all of us. It might refer to leaving a relationship or a job—or perhaps
to preparing to die or to remake oneself in a new image. It is impor-
tant to read Delgado's poem not merely as a statement coming from
a Latino poet but as a poetic statement framed in a Latino experi-
ence that can become a metaphor for any reader.

Throughout this book I've chosen poems that come from
many of the traditions and cultures that make up our society, but
I've chosen to write about them as poetry while helping the
reader orient him- or herself to many different perspectives on
experiences. A poem comes from the heart of the poet's experi-
ence, but it can go to the heart of any of our experiences. The
underground connections that poetry makes come not merely
from the way language is formed and shaped on the page and

through the spoken voice, but also from the heart of human experience, which I believe is translatable—sometimes with difficulty, but often with power.

It is a mistake to put poets in boxes and cut yourself off from poetic voices that might come from different perspectives and cultures than your own. A poet is not a preacher or a politician. At its finest, poetry tries to get at the heart of things through an intimate and imaginative crafting of the experience of the poet. To limit yourself to any one kind of poetry is to shut yourself down, to close yourself not merely to other voices but to the power of your own voice. I have found that reading widely and encountering poets whose experience is not mine and whose thoughts, ideas, sentiments, and affirmations are not my own is a growing experience. Learning to listen to other people's voices provides me with the opportunity to expand my own.

For example, this short poem by Martin Espada, "Julio Signing His Name," can apply to any immigrant people or others who work with their hands and choose to stand up for their rights. It reminds me of my grandfather, who was a carpenter, but also of many of my students who were schooled for work but not for contentious and dangerous lawsuits in defense of their rights.

> Julio cheats
> signing his name,
> copying slowly
> from his Social Security card,
> man's hand
> scratching letters child-crooked.
>
> But Julio's black hand
> was schooled for lettuce-picking,
> not lawsuits.

The following poem by Sherman Alexie has an intriguing structure. The first and last lines frame the poem. The rest is a parenthesis, and understanding this helps frame the reading of the work. The poem is shaped like this:

> I open the door
> . . . .
> . . . .
> . . . . etc.
> and invite the wind inside.

The poem is particular to the Native American experience and is ironic (it's called "The Exaggeration of Despair") and bitter, telling harsh truths and avoiding self-pity at the same time. Reading it can provide an entry into another person's experience, a confirmation of one's own experience, an affirmation of hope or a statement of cynical despair. There are many different perspectives that people bring to their reading of poems, and there is no single way to experience or interpret a poem, just as there is no ideal reader. We read through the masks of our own knowledge, desires, and experience, and the more open we are to being moved and educated by the words of others, the more poetry can be a vehicle for our growth.

The Exaggeration of Despair

I open the door
(this Indian girl writes that her brother tried to hang himself
with a belt just two weeks after her other brother did hang
himself

and this Indian man tells us that, back in boarding school, five priests
took him into a back room and raped him repeatedly

and this homeless Indian woman begs for quarters, and when I ask
her about the tribe, she says she's horny and bends over in front of me

and this Indian man dies in a car wreck on the same road
as his older brother, his younger brother, and the middle brother

and this homeless Indian man is the uncle of an Indian man
who writes for a large metropolitan newspaper, and so I know
them both

and this Indian child cries when he sits to eat at our table
because he had never known his family to sit at the same table

and this Indian poet shivers beneath the freeway
and begs for enough quarters to buy a pencil and paper

and this fancydancer passes out at the powwow
and wakes up naked, with no memory of the evening, all of
his regalia gone

and this is my sister, who waits years for an eagle, receives it
and stores it with our cousins, who then tell her it has
disappeared

and this is my father, whose own father died on Okinawa, shot
by a Japanese soldier who must have looked so much like him

and this is my father, whose mother died of tuberculosis
not long after he was born, and so my father must hear
coughing ghost

and this is my grandmother who saw, before the white man
came,
three ravens with white necks, and knew our God was going to
change)

and invite the wind inside.

Sometimes the form of a poem reveals very little about its con-
tent or the author's intent. But often there are other ways to orient
oneself to the poem. In the case of this poem by Charles Simic, the
title becomes essential to the meaning of the poem. It is not the
first line, but it sets the context. We are in the neighborhood of a
packinghouse, in Simic's case in Chicago, and he is a student.

Slaughterhouse Flies
Evenings, they ran their bloody feet
Over the pages of my schoolbooks.
With eyes closed, I can still hear
The trees on our street
Saying a moody farewell to summer,

And someone, under our window, recalling
The silly old cows hesitating,
Growing suddenly suspicious
Just as the blade drops down on them.

It often helps to figure out the context and setting for a poem, for often the poet won't tell a story the way a novelist or historian will. Poetry proceeds by condensation. Sentences don't have to be complete; you aren't introduced to a full description of the character or place of the poem. The brush strokes are quick, often condensed, sometimes so personal and implicit that it takes a scholar or friend of the poet to decipher them. However, often there are hints, as in this poem. All one needs to know is that there is a slaughterhouse nearby and that the blood on the flies' feet is not just a flight of poetic fantasy. But that's not all there is to it—how many bloody feet have walked across our textbooks and lives? The poet lets the reader figure that out.

Here's a very different poem by Simic, one set in the bedroom at a different stage of his life. There is little I can say about it that it doesn't say for itself.

The Road in the Clouds
Your undergarments and mine,
Sent flying around the room
Like a storm of white feathers
Striking the window and ceiling.

Something like repressed laughter
Is in the air
As we lie in sweet content
Drifting off to sleep
With the treetops in purple light

And the sudden memory
Of riding a bicycle
Using no hands
Down a steep winding road
To the blue sea.

Here's a poem by George Oppen to look at and read. Notice the
way in which every stanza but the first begins toward the right-hand
margin. It requires a shift in perception, a new way of looking at the
text and reading it. Also think about the ways in which it might rep-
resent the hidden deer, the bedding down mentioned in the first
stanza. Also notice the ways in which sentences are broken, the ways
in which the lines diverge from prose and force the reader to shift
emphasis and attention. The lengths of the lines change and yet the
poem has a rhythm that fits with the content of the work and the puz-
zling, moving lines in the last stanza, which move the poem from a
portrait to an affirmation of faith in the power of language and poetry.

Psalm
Veritas sequitur . . .

In the small beauty of the forest
The wild deer bedding down—
That they are there!

                         Their eyes
Effortless, the soft lips
Nuzzle and the alien small teeth
Tear at the grass
                         The roots of it
Dangle from their mouths
Scattering earth in the strange woods.
They who are there.
                         Their paths
Nibbled thru the fields,
the leaves that shade them
Hang in the distances
Of sun

                              The small nouns
         Crying faith
         In this in which the wild deer
         Startle, and stare out.

Following are three poems for you to encounter yourself, to
look at, read, reread, read out loud. The poems are followed by
some comments about them by their authors. In the next few
chapters elements occurring in all of the poems you have read so
far will be examined in greater detail as a way to help develop
the habit of reading poetry. But the best preparation to encoun-
tering these deeper aspects of reading poetry is to begin by read-
ing and struggling through a few poems by yourself.

Reason
Said, Pull her up a bit will you, Mac, I want to unload
there.
Said, Pull her up my rear end, first come first serve.
Said, Give her the gun, Bud, he needs a taste of his own
    bumper.
Then the usher came out and got into the act:

Said, Pull her up, pull her up a bit, we need this space,
sir.
Said, For God's sake, is this still a free country or what?
You go back and take care of Gary Cooper's horse
And leave me handle my own car.

Saw them unloading the lame old lady,
Ducked out under the wheel and gave her an elbow,
Said, All you needed to do was just explain;
Reason, Reason is my middle name.

"Reason" is a favorite one of my poems because I
like the idea of speech—not images, not ideas, not
music, but people talking—as the material from
which poetry is made. So much inert surface, so
many hidden depths, such systematic richness of

play in tone and color, with these I too easily become impatient in modern poetry, because I like the spare and active interplay of talk.

. . . I like to get as many unimportant syllables in a five-stress line as I possibly can. Then they can't be implicative.

And the accents of a limited and maybe slightly mis-placed pride interest me. Good strong true pride we need more of, and oblique accents of it at least sound out the right direction.

The Journey

I am looking for a past
I can rely
on in order to look to death
with equanimity.
What was given me: my mother's largeness
to protect me,
my father's regularity
in coming home from work
at night, his opening the door
silently and smiling,
pleased to be back
and the lights on
in all the rooms
through which I could run
freely or sit at ease
at the table and do my homework
undisturbed: love arranged
as order directed at the next day.
Going to bed was a journey.

"The Journey" was written in recollection of a period in my childhood when things at home and in the street and school were going well, without painful problems. It was a lovely period which in my mature years I began to appreciate as a key period in my life, giving me a way of life to work towards in my maturity. It was a signpost during the turmoil I was confronted with as an adult in politics, in business, and in domestic affairs. I could look back at that relatively calm and relaxed time as a goal to work towards in my adult life and as a kind of saving vision to keep me from becoming altogether despairing.

Notice that the writing has a kind of nostalgia towards the end of the poem and that the poem begins with a backward look and statement of need in midst of a barely disguised longing for death, which, as the poem progresses, becomes transformed into a celebration of peace and hope, the longing for death absorbed in the vision of the beautiful past.

The Goddess

She in whose lipservice
I passed my time,
whose name I knew, but not her face,
came upon me where I lay in Lie Castle!

Flung me across the room, and
room after room (hitting the wall, re-
bounding—to the last
sticky wall—wrenching away from it
pulled hair out!)
till I lay outside the outer walls!

There in cold air
Lying still where her hand had thrown me,
I tasted the mud that splattered my lips:
the seeds of a forest were in it,
asleep and growing! I tasted
her power!

The silence was answering my silence,
a forest was pushing itself
out of sleep between my submerged fingers.

I bit on a seed and it spoke on my tongue
of day that shone already among stars
in the water-mirror of low ground,

and a wind rising ruffled the lights:
she passed near me returning from the encounter,
she who plucked me from the close rooms,

without whom nothing
flowers, fruits, sleeps in season,
without whom nothing
speaks in its own tongue, but returns
lie for lie!

I believe that poems should so arise from the
sequence of the poet's experience that their relation
to each other in the pattern of that experience
makes it impossible for him to think, or to wish to
think, of "a single favorite poem." One may feel—
and one most often feels this way about one's most
recent poem—that in one poem rather than another
one has said more and said it more precisely; but
these are superficial and fluctuating fondnesses. At
a deeper level one can no more favor one poem—
one part, that is, of the larger poem that is a life-
time's work-in-progress—than one can isolate other
elements and events of a life for preference: they
tend toward a whole, but as one cannot see the
design till it is done, one cannot know the value of
the parts or comprehend their interrelations except
as time passes. Perhaps one might say that the right
to choose a favorite among one's own poems is a

privilege of old age; or that only in old age does it truly become a possibility. Similarly, the reader who seriously studies a poet's works will find it more difficult to "prefer" the deeper his studies take him; even though he may make critical evaluations, technical distinctions, he will find himself led to accept, eventually, even those works that at first, before he came to know the whole work, seemed irrelevant, or unattractive to his "taste" because "taste" comes to seem a false, a superficial and pretentious, way of approach, itself irrelevant to the irreducible aliveness of a poem.

Nevertheless, I have chosen a poem not quite at random. I have chosen it because it is one that recalls to me one of those confrontations with Truth that every person, every soul, must sometimes experience if he or she is to live, to grow; and especially one who is a poet for poets have a genius for lying and an adoration for the truth, and it may be that the driving impulse of every poet is to maintain the dynamic interplay of these two passions.

2

It's the Breaks

The Attic Which Is Desire:
the unused tent
of

bare beams
beyond which

directly wait
the night

and day—
Here

from the street
by

```
    * * *
    * S *
    * O *
    * D *
    * A *
    * * *
```

ringed with
running lights

and darkened
pane

exactly
down the center

is
transfixed

Read this poem by William Carlos Williams a few times and
look at its shape as well. The poem is visual and verbal at the same
time. The way it looks on the page, the way in which the lines are
organized, and the sounds of the words all work together in complex
ways that provide an entry into some of the delights and complexi-
ties of contemporary poetry.

In the middle of the poem is a neon "SODA" sign ringed with
what he refers to as "running lights." The poem is about desire,
which is equated with an attic. The lines are short, broken, incom-
plete, separated. The poem begins with a small letter, "t," and
does not end with a period. The language is condensed, and the
final picture is of the tent of an attic transfixed behind a SODA
sign—a portrait of a room holding memories and relics of the past
framed by the shining and blinking lights calling to new pur-
chases—a portrait of desire. The question is, how to read this
poem? How to scan it for oneself, to say it out loud, to take it in?

One way is to think of the poem as a song and look for the
breaks and the silences. My son, who is a conductor and com-
poser, talks about the importance of playing the breaks and the
silences. What he means is understanding how to use the pauses
between musical phrases, how to use the moment of a rest in a
piece to shape the tone and sentiment of the whole. Contemporary
poets play the breaks—within lines and between lines and stan-
zas—the way musicians play the pauses and the transitions from
one rhythm and style to another. When Williams chooses a line

with one word or a break in a thought, he is helping the reader shape the poem in her or his mind and voice. Consider the first two stanzas:

> the unused tent
> of
>
> bare beams
> beyond which

"The unused tent" is the attic of the title of the poem, and the unused desire resides there. "Of" stands alone, especially followed by a new stanza that does not represent a new sentence or even a new phrase. The poet is slowing the reader down, and in "beyond which" takes the reader out of the attic into the night and day in the next stanza and the sign below in the one after that. The poem moves easily from the abstract to the concrete through pauses and breaks, through transitions that are made coherent to the reader by the way in which lines are divided and stanzas separated.

William Carlos Williams was a pioneer in freeing poetry to play with the length of a line and the use of pauses and spaces to create what I like to call poetic density—the shifting, complex reality that does not have to adhere to the linear rules of grammar and logic. Here is a poem by Robert Duncan in which pauses within lines, breaks of lines themselves, and the physical shaping of the whole lead me, at least, to a rending emotional experience, an identification with the poet's suffering, the power of love, and the regeneration of life in ways that a formal description of the events could never do. It makes sense to look at the poem before reading it, to get a sense of where the breaks are, and as you read to respect the way in which the poet helps you read the poem through his pauses and silences. Notice how the title sets the context for the poem and is therefore part of the poem itself. Titles of poems should never be ignored.

After a Long Illness

No faculty not   ill at ease
let us
begin where I must

from the failure of systems   breath
less,   heart
and lungs water-logd.

Clogged with light chains   the kidneys'
condition is terminal   life

the light and the heavy, the light
and dark.   It has always been
close upon a particular Death, un
disclosed   what's behind

seeing, feeling, tasting, smelling   —that Cloud!

For two years
bitterness pervaded:

in the physical body   the high blood pressure
the accumulation of toxins, the
break-down of ratios,

in the psyche   "stewed in its own juices"
the eruption of hatreds,   the prayer
—I didn't have a prayer—   your care
alone kept my love clear.

I will be there again   the ways
must become crosst   and again
dark passages,   dangerous straits.

My Death attended me and I knew
I was not going to die,
nursed me thru.   Life took hold.
What I ate   I threw up
and crawled thru as if turned inside out.

Every thought I had I saw
sickened me.   Secretly
in the dark   the filters
of my kidneys   petrified   and my Death
rearranged the date He has with me.

The first line begins with a pause:

No faculty not   ill at ease

The space between "not" and "ill at ease" is ill at ease. The
poem begins in pain, with disease and dying. The lack of compro-
mise in this first line and in the first three lines together set the
presence of death at the center of the poem:

No faculty not   ill at ease
let us
begin where I must

The two negatives in the first line—something schoolchildren
are told is not grammatical—are essential here. No system is not in
trouble. Not the more grammatical "Every system is in trouble."
The "no" and "not" emphasize the stress on the body Duncan
feels, the total lack of well-being. This leads to

from the failure of systems   breath
less,   heart
and lungs water-logd.

> Clogged with light chains   the kidneys'
> condition is terminal   life

The intensity of this poem comes from Duncan's language, but also from the way he chooses to use spacing and the breaks to shape the grammatical structure, both within and between lines and stanzas. It is as if the poet were providing the reader not merely with a written text, but with a musical score to decipher, read once, read again as the meaning sinks in, and then sing or read aloud. The rereading of a poem is part of the act of reading it and perhaps essential to internalizing and coming to love it. However, I admit that not all poems bear up upon rereading, nor do all of them tempt a second, much less a third and fourth reading. It is a matter of taste and emotion, of what moves you enough to make the effort to mine a poem for the riches it might contain.

Playing around with familiar nursery rhymes can provide insight into what breaking a line or making breaks within a line can do to transform the meaning and impact of a poem. Here's a simple rhyming verse (lines 1 and 2, *play* and *day*; lines 3 and 4 the almost-rhyme, called an off-rhyme, *sleep* and *street*; and lines 5 and 6, *call* and *all*. According to Iona and Peter Opie in their classic collection *The Oxford Dictionary of Nursery Rhymes,* "the American folklorist Newell wrote (1883): 'In the last generation children still sang in our towns [this] ancient summons to evening sports.'"

> Boys and girls come out to play,
> The moon doth shine as bright as day.
> Leave your supper and leave your sleep,
> And join your playfellows in the street.
> Come with a whoop and come with a call,
> Come with good will or not at all.

This innocent verse can be restructured by changing spacing and line breaks and adding a few type changes to tell a thoroughly different story:

Boys
>>> and
>>>>> **girls**
>>>>>>> come out
>>> to **play,**
The moon doth shine asbrightasday.
Leave
>>>> your supper and
>> leave
>>>> your sleep,

And join your playfellows
>>>>> **in the street.**
>>>> Come with a whoop and
>>>>>> come with a call,
>> Come with good will or not
>>>>> at all.

This somewhat crude change in the shape of the poem
draws the reader to the bold type and away from the rhyme. So
instead of the play/day, sleep/street, and call/all axes, the
bold type leads the eye: boys, girls, play, in the street. This
loss of innocence in the message changes the poem from one
of sanctioned kid play to defiance and sexual encounter. The
pauses and line breaks emphasize this change in meaning and
tone. Here's an example of another childhood rhyme, one that
I remember one of my aunts taught me when I was three or four:

One misty, moisty morning,
When cloudy was the weather,
There I met an old man
Clothed all in leather;
Clothed all in leather,
with cap under his chin.
"How do you do," and "How do you do,"
And "How do you do?" again!

And here is a version that changes the line breaks and spac-ing with the intent of changing the very nature of the poem. The leather in the original poem was a raincoat worn by a fisherman in a storm. The leather of the revised version has a different meaning.

I
One misty,
     moisty,
         morning,
When cloudy was the
               weather,
There I met an old man

Clothed all
             in leather;
Clothed all
      in leather,

with cap under his chin.
How do you do,
  and how do you
           do,

And how do
    you
      do
         again?

Recently I discovered a wonderful series of rewritings of "Mary Had a Little Lamb" by the poet and essayist Judson Jerome. They are in his book *The Poet and the Poem.*

Mary	Mary had a	mar yhAD a (lit)le
had a little lamb	little lamb its	1, AM(bit)s
its fleece	fleece was white as	(flee) cew as w(hit)e
was white	snow and	ass(no)
as snow	everywhere that	w, AND EVE
and everywhere	Mary went her	r, y, W (hER) Et
that Mary went	lamb was sure to	(hA)t
her lamb	go	Mar ywen
was sure		thE,r lambwaSS
to go.		ure
		TOgO

Jerome comments on his revisions:

> Line units are the most pervasive characteristic of all
> poetry, and it is not a simple matter in our day for a
> poet to decide where one line ought to end and the
> next begin. Some poets employ instinct. They have
> no fixed principle, but divide when they feel the
> urge. We have mingling traditions—units deter-
> mined by number of stresses as in Anglo-Saxon verse
> and units determined by number of syllables. . . . the
> most common practice is to mingle the two, creating
> accentual-syllabic verse in which the units are met-
> rical feet. . . . of course, a variety of principles . . .
> can be used with good effect. The three versions of
> Mary I gave at the beginning, though written in par-
> ody, can be used to illustrate techniques which can
> actually be quite useful.

> Notice first of all how important the line divisions are.
> Each gives a decidedly different emotional tone and
> effect to the words—because although we read right
> on, the line units make a momentary impression; we
> get the impact of the line and then of the sentences
> and rhetorical units. The first example breaks after
> significant words so that each line seems to arrive, to

climb to a minor crest. That is, the lines can be made to emphasize the phrases or thought units or to pull against them.

The second example is based on an opposite principle. The significant words occur at the beginnings of the lines and the last words are all dropped, thrown away, the voice trailing off. Beginnings and endings of lines are the spots for natural emphases, and the endings are usually stronger. By deliberately de-emphasizing them, one gets an interestingly jerky, indifferent tone, a modern slur, shying from emotion and rhetoric.

Apologies to [e. e.] cummings for the third. While it may look silly, actually it is a kind of tribute—for he has taught us so much about the nature of words, punctuation, space, the nature of language, that we cannot use his lessons without seeming to parody him or imitate him too slavishly. Just as much modern painting fragments experience, vision, shape to make us really see it, make us aware of color and texture and form, so he fragmented language—and with an illuminating explosion. My version of "Mary" can be used to illustrate some of the possibilities.

Since our perception of punctuation, for example, had become dulled by habit, he put it to new uses. Here, for example, the capitalized letters (as sometimes in cummings) spell out a kind of anagram message: ADAM AND EVE WERE A MESS, TOO. Well, once we begin thinking about Adam and Eve in relation to that lamb and Mary, our minds become open to all sorts of things—from a more sacred Mary and sacred lamb to the bawdier implications of the first line. In cummings one would expect the various words within words, spaces, juxtapositions, interruptions and meldings to have some relevance to the poem's purpose (however difficult that relevance may be to discover). Here, I confess, they are somewhat arbitrary, although you might have fun considering them. Fun is a valuable part of the experience; it would be a great mistake to read cummings deadpan. It would also be a mistake to expect to be able to put all the various innuendoes and side effects of such a poem into a logical paraphrase. The method forces you to see the poem as a thing, an art object, no more subject to restatement than would be a statue.

Also, notice, it forces you to see. Poetry is primarily an auditory experience, but since most people come in contact with it on paper, there is ample reason for making it a visual experience as well. Though many poets, old and new, have experimented with its visual possibilities (writing poems like circles or wings or altars or diamonds or mirror images, or including various kinds of anagrams), no one has to the same extent as cummings made the written poem so much a part of its essential being. Many of his poems can be effectively read aloud—he has a magnificent lyric gift; but others cannot be read aloud at all, their meaning is so inextricable from their shape on the page.

Here's a poem by e. e. cummings from the volume *1x1* that illustrates Jerome's comments:

XXXI
a-

float on some
?
i call twilight you

'll see

```
an in
-ch
of an if

&

who
is
the

)

more
dream than become
more

am than imagine
```

The poet Denise Levertov, whom you have already encountered in this book, also provides insight into the importance of line breaks, which she considers as part of the modern poets' redefinition of what she describes as "a peculiarly poetic, alogical, parallel (not competitive) punctuation."

> . . . there is at our disposal no tool of the poetic craft more important, none that yields more subtle and precise effects, than the line break if it is properly understood.

> If I say that its function in the development of modern poetry in English is evolutionary I do not mean to imply that I consider modern, nonmetrical poetry "better" or "superior" to the great poetry of the past, which I love and honor. That would obviously be absurd. But I do feel that there are few poets today whose sensibility naturally expresses itself in the traditional form (except for satire or pronounced

irony), and that those who do so are somewhat anachronistic. The closed, contained quality of such forms has less relation to the relativistic sense of life which unavoidably prevails in the late twentieth century than modes that are more exploratory, more open ended. A sonnet may end with a question; but its essential, underlying structure arrives at *resolution*. "Open forms" do not necessarily terminate inconclusively, but their degree of conclusion is— structurally, and thereby expressively—less pronounced, and partakes of the open quality of the whole. . . . The forms more apt to express the sensibility of our age are the exploratory, open ones.

In what way is contemporary, nonmetrical poetry exploratory? What I mean by that word is that such poetry, more than most poetry of the past, incorporates and reveals the *process* of thinking/feeling, feeling/thinking, rather than focusing more exclusively on its *results*; and in so doing it explores (or can explore) human experience in a way that is not wholly new but is (or can be) valuable in its subtle difference of approach: valuable both as human testimony and as aesthetic experience. And the crucial precision tool for creating this exploratory mode is the line break. The most obvious function of the linebreak is rhythmic: it can record the slight (but meaningful) hesitations between word and word that are characteristic of the mind's dance among perceptions but which are not noted by grammatical punctuation. Regular punctuation is a part of regular sentence structure, that is, of the expression of completed thoughts; and this expression is typical of prose, even though prose is not at all times bound by its logic. But in poems one has the opportunity not only, as in expressive prose, to depart from the syntactic norm, but to make manifest, by an intrinsic structural means, the interplay or counterpoint of process and completion—in other words, to present the dynamics of perception *along with* its arrival at full expression. The linebreak is a form of punctuation additional to the punctuation that forms part of the logic of completed thoughts. Line breaks—together with intelligent use of indentation and other devices of scoring—represent a peculiarly *poetic*, alogical, parallel (not competitive) punctuation.

What is the nature of the alogical pauses the linebreak records? If readers will think of their own speech, or their silent inner monologue, when describing thoughts, feelings, perceptions, scenes or events, they will, I think, recognize that they frequently hesitate—albeit very briefly—as if with an unspoken question,—a "what?" or a "who?" or a "how?"—before nouns, adjectives, verbs, adverbs, none of which require to be preceded by a comma or other regular punctuation in the course of syntactic logic. To incorporate these pauses in the rhythmic structure of the poem can do several things: for example, it allows the reader to share more intimately the experience that is being articulated; and by introducing an alogical counter-rhythm into the logical rhythm of syntax it causes, as they interact, an effect closer to song than to statement, closer to dance than to walking. . . .

Here's a vivid example of using line breaks to shape the meaning and rhythm of a poem. In William Carlos Williams's "The Locust Tree in Flower," each line consists of just one word.

Among
of
green

stiff
old
bright

broken
branch
come

white
sweet
May

again

The connections between the lines are not grammatical, nor is the whole, which can be read as a single nongrammatical sentence:

Among of green stiff old bright broken branch come
white sweet May again.

However, the poem reads differently from the sentence and reveals its meaning through this reading. Its simple power comes across if you recite it out loud several times, adjusting your reading, and the meaning becomes clearer to you.

Each stanza groups three words, and the whole builds to a delightful sense of the renewal of life. Out of the green stiff old bright broken branch comes a beautiful white flower–again. The last word transforms the whole. This is not merely birth, but renewal. Williams understates his meaning. This is not a treatise on spring. It is more like an intimate landscape, a reminder of how new growth continually emerges from old life.

William Carlos Williams was a friend, teacher, and inspiration to Allen Ginsberg. I'm sure that Ginsberg had read all of Williams's poetry and that when he wrote the following poem, the form of the poem, the line breaks, and the sentiments were a response to and elaboration of "The Locust Tree in Flower," for the coming of spring is a powerful and traditional metaphor for the awakening of desire. Notice that Ginsberg was playing the line breaks just as his mentor did in this particular poem, whose title acknowledges dual authorship and is a tribute from a student to a teacher.

    Written in My Dream by W. C. Williams
    "As Is
    you're bearing

    a common
    Truth

    Commonly Known
    as desire

    No need
    to dress

    it up
    as beauty

    No need
    to distort

    what's not
    standard
    to be
    understandable.

    Pick your
    nose

    eyes ears
    tongue

    sex and
    brain

to show
the populace

Take your
chances

on
your accuracy

Listen to
yourself

talk to
yourself

and others
will also

gladly
relieved

of the burden-
their own

thought
and grief.
What began
as desire

will end
wiser."

Here's a poem by John Taggart in which spacing, the placement of words on the page, and the use of empty space and pauses are used to reflect, in language, the music of Thelonius Monk. It is a version of the hymn "Abide With Me," which according to legend was sung when the *Titanic* was sinking.

It is reminiscent of e. e. cummings's use of spacing, although it is clearly meant to be spoken or sung and not just appreciated for its spatial form on the page.

Monk
   1
A-bide   a-   a-

bide

     fast falls
     the   tide

     fast

the darkness deepens.

   2

     with abide

     with

When others   fail

              fail

              fail

    comforts flee

   fail   flee

abide with me

abide with me

    me   me

Learning to read line breaks helps make reading poetry more like speaking with inflection and expression than droning on in a monotone voice. However, poetry is not casual speech and line breaks provide a more formal structure to the language of poetry than conversation. Poems are dual—meant to be read and meant to be spoken. However, they are more like classical music than like jazz—there is a written score, and the improvisations take place within the constraints of the text. They have to do with inflection, emphasis, interpretation. Of course, many poets love to improvise at poetry slams and contests, but the written poem is fixed and its reading is usually done within the limits of the text. The line breaks and the spacing are part of the score, to be neglected at the peril of losing the meaning, rhythm, and impact of the whole.

This poem by Ron Padgett, though its general shape is more conventional than the last few poems, depends as much upon the line breaks for its coherence and effect as they do. The title sets the scene for the poem: "Disgruntled" is a cranky word that sets the reader up for a disgruntling experience. Yet Padgett, as is usual in his poetry, has a wry, ironic, and humorous take on disgruntlement as well as most everything else.

Disgruntled Man
I brush the hair located on the right side of my head,
I brush it beautifully,
thinking of you. Then
I notice that the hair on the left side
is standing slightly higher than on the right,
and my head appears to be lopsided.

I don't want it to look that way.
So I begin to brush down the left side,
grimly, with a sense of purpose
devoid of pleasure
that drips down the well wall
toward some deep, dark and cool pool
in which only peace is reflected.

> Soon my head is in balance,
> but it has become a head brushed for bad reasons
> and I do not like the face I see.
> A man disgruntled
> with the way he brushed his hair.

The first line is simple and straightforward, longish, and the second shorter line is highlighted by the word "beautifully." We can visualize the poet brushing his hair with grace, ease, and persistence. The third line implies he's doing it to please someone he cares about, and "then." The pause here takes the tale in another direction and ends with a lopsided look, discontent, almost disgruntlement. The line "devoid of pleasure" takes the poem in a different direction and the line break allows the reader to follow the poet down the "well wall" to where pleasure might be, and then, after a greater pause between the stanzas, the head is at last in balance but brushed for bad reasons. The flow of the story is controlled by the line breaks, and when read aloud or quietly in the bathroom while brushing one's own hair, the entire ritual of trying to make oneself attractive can be seen as a silly, self-deprecating, ultimately frustrating experience.

In this next poem, by Imamu Amiri Baraka, a more violent experience is dramatized and intensified by the way in which sentences are jammed up in single poetic lines, and in which lines are broken, shortened, allowed to run into each other. The key to reading this poem is to extract the drama from the way the poet has chosen to shape the words, sentences, and phrases. It is not a matter of rhyme or regularity. The poet is trying to move the reader into the drama and make him or her experience the horror of violent death and murder. The words themselves ring with the force of gunshots and reinforce the structure of the lines. In the first paragraph the word "shot'" is repeated four times. The short, crackling language of the rest of the stanza reinforces that sense of horror and leads to the last phrase "to a full halt." The second stanza doesn't let the reader off the hook as it reiterates that the victim was "shot dead.'" In this poem the language and the lines all lead to a reenactment of an unambiguously horrible and violent event.

Incident

He came back and shot. He shot him. When he came
back, he shot, and he fell, stumbling, past the
shadow wood, down, shot, dying, dead, to full halt.

At the bottom, bleeding, shot dead. He died then, there
after the fall, the speeding bullet, tore his face
and blood sprayed fine over the killer and the grey light.

Pictures of the dead man are everywhere. And his spirit
sucks up the light. But he died in darkness darker than
his soul and everything tumbled blindly with him dying
down the stairs.

We have no word

on the killer, except he came back, from somewhere
to do what he did. And shot only once into his victim's
stare, and left him quickly when the blood ran out. We know
the killer was skillful, quick, and silent, and that the victim
probably knew him. Other than that, aside from the caked sourness
of the dead man's expression, and the cool surprise in the fixture

of his hands and fingers, we know nothing.

Here's another example of how line breaks shape the reading
and understanding of a poem. Jane Hirshfield's unlikely subject is
simply a room and what it does and does not do. Notice the length
of lines, the places where pauses shift attention, the breaks in
stanzas that call for longer pauses. This is a good poem to work
one's way into slowly.

A Room

A room does not turn its back on grief.
Anger does not excite it.
Before desire, it neither responds
nor draws back in fear.

Without changing expression,
it takes
and gives back;
not a tuft in the mattress alters.

Windowsills evenly welcome
both heat and cold.
Radiators speak or fall silent as they must.

Doors are not equivocal,
floorboards do not hesitate or startle.
Impatience does not stir the curtains,
a bed is neither irritable nor rapacious.

Whatever disquiet we sense in a room
we have brought there.

And so I instruct my ribs each morning,
pointing to hinge and plaster and wood—
　　You are matter, as they are.
　　See how perfectly it can be done.
　　Hold, one day more, what is asked.

Notice the indentation of the last stanza, which represents a
shift from talking about the room to the voice of the poet instructing
her ribs. There is a change of voice indicated here, a change in tone,
and in a way a summary of the meaning of the poem, which has to do
with not merely the way rooms contain human life and yet are a con-
tainer of life rather than actors in it, but the way in which people
might learn steadiness and persistence from the rooms we live in.

The line breaks and pauses here and in many contemporary
poems shape the drama and argument of the work. They are not
incidental to the language and the images but score them, orches-
trate them, and turn them into drama and living speech.

Here's another example, this time by the poet June Jordan, of a
poem in which the shaping of the lines and the breaking of the stanzas

create the rhythm of the tale. This poem makes the reader into a voyeur, a witness to a small and important event. There is something very gentle and loving about the poet's approach to her subject, to her readers.

> *If You Saw a Negro Lady*
> If you saw a Negro lady
> sitting on a Tuesday
> near the whirl-sludge doors of
> Horn & Hardart on the main drag
> of downtown Brooklyn
>
> solitary and conspicuous as plain
> and neat as walls impossible to
> fresco and you watched her self-
> conscious features shape about
> a Horn & Hardart teaspoon
> with a pucker from a cartoon
> she would not understand
> with spine as straight and solid
> as her years of bending over floors
>
> allowed
> skin cleared of interest by a ruthless
> soap   nails square and yellowclean
> from metal files
>
> sitting in a forty-year-old flush
> of solitude and prickling
> from the new white cotton blouse
> concealing nothing she had ever noticed
> even when she bathed and never
> hummed a bathtub tune nor knew one
>
> If you saw her square
> above the dirty
> mopped-on antiseptic floors
> before the rag-wiped table tops

little finger   broad and stiff
in heavy emulation of a cockney

mannerism

would you turn her treat
into surprise observing
happy birthday

The poem ends with a question for the reader that begs the reader to go back and read again, to take in the story one more time and then feel the event and rethink it. The birthday is a surprise, but it is also an invitation to rethink one's own perceptions and to reread and become more intimate with the poem. The lines guide the reading, help with the pacing, provide a way for the reader to orient her-or himself to the more complex meanings of the poem.

Reading poetry is not a rushed activity. It is not a question of how quickly one can read or how many poems one can read at a sitting. It is a more meditative experience, and a more reflective one as well. Poems can be taken in through rereading and through simply letting them sink in. I find it useful and very moving sometimes to read the same poem every day for a week, or to return to a book of poems I don't quite get a few weeks after a first reading. A reader can hover around poetry as taste develops, and can always dip in for a moment and sometimes spend concentrated time. But one does not have to get through poems to the end as one does with mystery novels or biographies. Reading poetry is a much more nonlinear experience, and an ongoing one. I find it impossible to throw out or give away a book of poetry that has intrigued, challenged, or moved me because I know I will probably return to it someday either as an old friend or as something I do not fully understand and can learn more from.

Finally, here is a poem by Al Young with lines of one, two, three, four, five, six, and eight words in length. They are scored like music, mixed according to the flow of the poet's reflections and sentiments, shaped skillfully like an art song. Have fun with them.

A Song for Little Children
Always it's either
a beginning
or some end:
the baby's being born
or its parents are
dying, fading on
like the rose
of the poem withers, its light going out
while gardens come in
to bloom

Let us stand on streetcorners
in the desolate era
& propose a new kind
of crazyness

Let us salute one another
one by one
two by two the soft belly
moving toward
the long sideburns
the adams apple
or no apple at all

Let there be
in this crazyness
a moon
a violin
a drum

Let the beautiful brown girl
join hands with
her black sister
her golden sister
her milkskinned sister
their eternal wombs
turning with the moon

Let there be a flute
to squeal above
the beat & the bowing
to open us up
that the greens
the blues
the yellows
the reds
the silvers &
indescribable rusts
might flow out
amazingly
& blend
with the wind

Let the wobbly spin
of the earth
be a delight

wherein
a caress forms
the most perfect circle

Let the always be love
the beginning be love
love the only
possible
end

3

Rhythm and Melody

An Ear for Poetry

Why I Am a Poet
My father's gravestone said, "I knew it was time."
Our house was alive. It moved,
it had song. The singers back home
all stood in rows along the railroad line.
When the wind came along the track
every neighbor sang. In the last
house I followed the wind—it
left the world and went on.
We knew, the wind and I, that space
ahead of us, the world like an empty room.
I looked back where the sky came down.
Some days no train would come.
Some birds didn't have a song.

Reading poetry out loud can seem difficult, even embarrassing. I spend part of the time living on eleven acres in a rural community and can go out and sing and shout whenever I like without being considered disruptive, crazy, or a public nuisance. On the other hand, when I am in the city, if I speak a poem I don't do it outside or in the hall, but in the privacy of my apartment or sometimes with friends at a picnic or on a hike. And I have learned to read poetry and listen to my own internalized voice so that poems can accompany me on an airplane or be my lunchtime reading.

Learning to read a poem is like learning to sing. It has to do with following the complex rhythms of the verse, savoring the language, and engaging the sensuous surfaces of the words, their look and their sounds. It means letting constellations of sounds and phrases have a weight as well as letting the meaning and imagery of a poem sink in. This means, in Judson Jerome's phrase, developing "an ear for poetry"; learning how to read not merely the words of a poem, but its flow and movement.

In the poem "Why I Am a Poet," William Stafford equates poetry with song and himself with the wind (the train) from the outside that moves people to sing. The relationship between written and spoken poetry and song is complex, and the boundary between poems and songs is not fixed. There are song lyrics that can be recited and read as poems; there are poems that can be sung. For example, Allen Ginsberg has set some William Blake poems to music and recorded them; Eddie Palmieri has orchestrated and performed poems by Victor Hernández Cruz; and Anne Sexton performed her poems to the accompaniment of a high school rock band. Of course, there are also traditional musical settings of poetry, the most notable of which are Beethoven's setting of Schiller's "Ode to Joy" at the end of the Ninth Symphony and Schubert's, Schumann's, Mendelssohn's, and Lizst's settings of poems by Heinrich Heine. Poetry is meant to be heard and spoken in rhythms and with an expression that approximates song. At the same time, it is spoken, not sung. However, the fine line between reading poetry and singing it is not fixed or clear. Some poets, when they read their works, chant. Others speak in slow, almost inaudible voices that put subtle emphases and inflections on the words of the poems. There are poets who shout, poets who mumble, poets who dance when they read, and poets who move only their mouths. What I see in common, however, is that the emphasis is on the language and the image, with the rhythm and melody in a poem playing essential enhancing roles. Except in the case of poets who read to the accompaniment of live music, such as jazz and hip-hop poets, the music never takes over. The language is central.

Langston Hughes drew inspiration for a number of his poems from the blues and other song forms. In this poem rhyme and rhythm are used to set up a beat, and the poem, while never set to music and intended to be read, not sung, straddles the border between song and poetry. It could, however, be set to music. There is in addition to rhyme and rhythm a melody here, something that moves up and down and in and out.

Border Line
I used to wonder
About living and dying—
I think the difference lies
Between tears and crying.

I used to wonder
About here and there—
I think the distance
Is nowhere.

Hughes said of this poem:

"Border Line" is one of my favorite poems because it seems to carry within itself a melody which I can hear although I cannot sing a note. Since this poem is like a song, its sound conditioned its saying. What it says is therefore so much of a piece with the way it is said that form and content are one, like a circle whose shape is itself and whose self is its shape, and which could be no other way to be what it is. . . .

After a first reading the rhyme clues make a second reading more fluent and musical, melodic, while making the content and feelings in the poem more transparent.

Rhymes are clues to the overall rhythm and structure of a poem that are not available in most contemporary poetry. There are other clues in poems, however, that help the reader get a sense of how the poem scans, how it sounds, how one can read it and speak it. Line breaks are an essential way to understand and enter the rhythm and melody of a poem. It is important to understand the distinction between rhythm and melody in a poem. You can set up a rhythm, a beat, but still read the poem in a monotone with no accent or expression. The melody of a poem has to do with the way in which it is inflected. Think, for example, of these sentences:

This is Dick.

This is Jane.

This is Spot.

See Dick and Jane run.

See Spot run.

The line breaks (actually page breaks in the first grade reader I had in school) let you know when to pause. They indicate a larger unit and set up the rhythm of the primer. Children fall into the line-by-line reading and begin to get a sense of the sentence as a unit of thought. Alhough this is not the most creative way to teach reading, it is illustrative of the way in which even simple primers like this use some of the techniques of poetry. Dick and Jane can be transformed without changing the line breaks or breaking the rhythms. Read, or even better say out loud, these five lines word by word in a bored tone, stopping for line breaks. Then read them as if the accompanying picture were taken in wartime and the children and the dog were fleeing an invading army. Imagine the kinds of illustrations that could accompany such a book. Then read them a third time in a scornful tone, as if there were a question mark instead of a period at the end of the first three lines and as if the fourth and fifth line indicated cowardice. This variation in inflection and expression is what I mean by the melody of a poem. It is not separate from the rhythm, but adds a human voice to the beat and structure.

Denise Levertov, some of whose poems have already appeared in this book, talks about this melodic aspect of a poem and its relationship to line breaks in the following way:

> *How* do the linebreaks affect the melodic element of a poem? So simply that it seems amazing that this aspect of their function is disregarded—yet not only student poetry workshops but any magazine or anthology of contemporary poetry provides evidence of a general lack of understanding of this factor; and even when individual poets manifest an intuitive sense of how to break their lines it seems rarely to be accompanied by any theoretical comprehension of what they've done right. Yet it is not hard to demonstrate to students that—given that the deployment of the poem on the page is regarded as a score, that is, as the visual instructions for auditory effects—the way the lines are broken affects not only rhythm but *pitch patterns*.
>
> Rhythm can be sounded on a monotone, a single pitch; melody is the result of pitch patterns combined with rhythmic patterns. The way in which linebreaks, observed respectfully, as a part of a score (and regarded as, say, roughly a half comma in duration), determine the pitch pattern of a sentence, can clearly be seen if a poem, or a few lines of it, is written out in a variety of ways (changing the line breaks but nothing else) and read aloud. Take, for instance, these lines of my own (picked at random):
>
> Crippled with desire, he questioned it.
> Evening upon the heights, juice of the pomegranate:
> who could connect it with sunlight?

Read them aloud. Now try reading the same words aloud from this score:

Crippled with desire, he
questioned it. Evening
upon the heights,
juice of the pomegranate:
who
could connect it with sunlight?

Or:

Crippled
with desire, he questioned
it. Evening
upon the heights, juice
of the pomegranate:
who could
connect it with sunlight?

Etc.

The intonation, the ups and downs of the voice, involuntarily changes as the rhythm (altered by the place where the tiny pause or musical "rest" takes place) changes. These changes could be recorded in graph form by some instrument, as heartbeats or brain waves are graphed. The point is not whether the lines, as I wrote them, are divided in the best possible way; as to that, readers must judge for themselves. I am simply pointing out that, read naturally but with respect for the line break's fractional pause, a pitch pattern change *does occur* with each variation of lineation. A beautiful example of expressive lineation is William Carlos Williams's well-known poem about the old woman eating plums:

They taste good to her.
They taste good
to her. They taste
good to her.

First the statement is made; then the word *good* is
(without the clumsy overemphasis a change of typeface
would give) brought to the center of our (and her)
attention for an instant; then the word *taste* is given
similar momentary prominence, with *good* sounding on
a new note, reaffirmed—so that we have first the gen-
eral recognition of well-being, then the intensification
of that sensation, then its voluptuous location in the
sense of taste. And all this is presented through indi-
cated pitches, that is, by melody, not by rhythm alone.

I have always been thrilled by the way in which the
musicality of a poem could arise from what I called
"fidelity to experience," but it took me some time to
realize what the mechanics of such precision were as
they related to this matter of pitch pattern.

Consider this poem by Chitra Banerjee Divakaruni. On your
first reading, pay attention to the line breaks. It would be best to
read it out loud.

The Babies: I
Again last night as we slept,
the babies
were falling from the sky.
So many of them——
eyes wide as darkness,
glowing lineless palms.
The dogs crooned their coming. The owls
flew up to them
on great dusty wings.

And all over the world
from beds hollow as boats
children held up
their silent scarred hands.

Now read the poem again, trying to shape the phrases and let the melody emerge. Do it slowly. For example, how should

the babies
were falling from the sky.

be phrased, and how should the next line, "So many of them—" be inflected? The "So many" is central. Not a few babies, but so many we can't number them. The poignancy of the poem has to be represented in the reading. And then there are dogs' voices, the owls' wings—both can be heard through the reading. And then the children holding up their scarred hands to the falling babies—the poem presents a single, dynamic, painful picture. The way in which the lines and stanzas are broken and their lengths varied are guides to how the poem should sound. On a third reading the poem takes its full shape and sound and can be read without thought to the breaks but with an expression of the content and passion the poet has shaped into the work. The melody in "The Babies: I" is not repetitious. It is one continuous line varied in tone, emotion, and inflection. This is a poem to be read as a whole, to be seen and understood as a whole. The melody is like the plaintive line of mourning that one finds in many funeral ceremonies.

It is not just the lines that shape this melody, but the sounds of the words. Although "slept," "sky," and "So" do not rhyme, the "s" sound frames the first four lines.

In the next lines there are also sounds that repeat. The dogs "crooned their coming," the "c" carrying the melody along. The "beds hollow as boats" again creates a resonance that becomes memorable and sayable. These repetitions culminate in a final repetition, "silent scarred hands." The poem's melody is shaped by the sounds of words and clusters of words, and as you read your way into it, it makes sense to pause over them, read a line or a few lines before returning to the whole poem. I find that this helps develop not only an understanding of the poem but also an understanding of my own voice and ways of clustering sounds and shaping my ideas and feelings in language.

Another poem that centers on babies, this one by Janice Mirikitani, has a very different melodic and rhythmic structure, and a very different sense of bitterness and pain. Read it, silently at first, then out loud. I'll save my comments until after you have a chance to enter into the poem.

Cry

For the ten infants buried at Tule
Lake who died
during the incarceration of
Japanese Americans during
WWII and to those artists and
activists in the Northwest
Asian Communities
who in 1990 erected new
graves to keep their
memory alive.

There are knives in the child's crib.
Blades of desert wind
cut the cord from its mother's
womb,
a chain of dust
around its throat.
Matsubara Baby, Tetsuno Kiyono,
Yamamoto Baby.

When the stone speaks
we will not forget
Okada Baby, Hirao Dick Nishizaki.
Perhaps in easier times
you would have lived.
Infants buried at Tule Lake.
Yamamuro Baby, George Uyeda,
Kazuo Harry Nishizaki, Loni Miyoko Toriumi,
Seki Baby.
Peonies plucked
by cruel weather, crushed into the sand,
suffocated in a jar with tight lid.

> *Your cry*
> *would have made*
> *the pain go away.*
> *I could have soothed*
> *with lullaby*
>
> > *hush little baby and when you wake*
> > *your mother will feed you omame*
> > *sleep little one and fret no more*
> > *your daddy's home from the war.*

Government made gravemarker,
makeshift, crumbling—
a cruel history,
all Japs are enemy aliens.
Infants?
buried
in concentration camps.
Something withers
starved of justice.

> *There is no meat or fish or milk*
> *rationed to rutabagas and potatoes,*
> *infirmaries smell of death.*
> *My breasts are dried*
> *and flat*
> *like this cracked earth*
> *beneath the barracks.*

The hot wind creeps
into my womb
and takes your breath.
The hot, barren desert wind
slices your hearts
severs your throats
before you could cry
or blossom.

Cry

We will
    carry you beyond these gates
    and barbed wire that encage us.
Run into the place
of live flowers,
walk the earth
with you to the ocean with its eternal
life, roaring for freedom,
comb your hair black like kelp
tied with bright red ribbons,
tell you about destinies that lie
before you vast as the orange horizon
    your arms
    reach like wings of astronauts,
    discoverers, peacemakers,
    singers, poets
    with breath and story.
We listen
as the wind with tongues
fires your name into stone

hush little baby and when you wake

We plant you
beneath gingko and pine,
fragrant cherry, quince,
where tall grasses
grow in a mist
that comes from the sea.
 Perpetual blooms
 will spring forth
 to remind us
 that you were born
 to be reborn
and our lips will whisper lullabyes

   sleep little one and fret no more.

In the middle
of the desert
protected from harsh wind
a new stone with mouth

cries.

  This poem has many melodies and is polyrhythmic. There is a lullaby, a lament, a chanting of names, a recounting of history, a personal expression of rage. The line breaks, the italic text, the placement of text on the page, the changing nature of the language the poet chooses for different parts of the poem are all guides for the reader. This poem has been read out loud many times in celebration of the event of the creation of new graves for the children who died in the Japanese internment camps. I have heard the poet read the poem in such ceremonial contexts as well as at poetry readings. The variation and tone–the lullaby voice, the angry voice, the ritual voice that she used—are not accessible to me. But I can read the poem and feel those changes, sing with the tone of lullabies I remember from my childhood. I can identify with the anger I feel about the Holocaust and all other events that stigmatize and damage a group of people simply because of their membership in the group. It also gets me to remembering ritual celebrations I experienced as a child in the Bronx in the 1940s. This poem resonates with reburials of people who died in the Holocaust, of burials of the American Civil War dead, of victims of slavery, of Native Americans' experience of genocide—and, crucially, of the baby victims, the ones who never had a chance to live. Here is yet another example of a poem that, though set in a particular cultural and historical context, is much larger. It will not be read in the same way by Japanese Americans who have experienced the Japanese removals and the camps as I might read it. But for all that, it is not a poem only for people whose families have experienced that. It is a poem whose central image and message are to all people who care about building a loving society. It can move all of us, not merely for what has happened to Japanese Americans but because of what we have experienced, what we have done to other peoples, and what has been done to us. It is another poem for the babies.

This poem by Pat Mora also refers to suffering children, but in a very different context. It is an attack on indifference. The line structure, the Spanish words in italics, and the placement of text on the page set up a dialogic structure that gives the reader a guide to reading. The stanzas placed on the right are answers, actually challenges, to what is said in the preceding stanzas that begin on the left side of the page. There are multiple melodies in this poem, dual rhythms that challenge the reader but also make the poem more complex and multivoiced. The poet does not tell you who is speaking, but shifts voices according to the logic of the poem and not the logic of prose. For me a first reading of a poem like this helps establish the melody, rhythm, and voices in the poem. Then I can reread it and give myself over more to the poet and her intent. This is the same for many contemporary poems: a preliminary reading of a poem helps orient you to the linguistic and structural choices the poet has made in order to reread the poem and relate more directly to its images, content, and sensibility.

Bilingual Christmas
Do you hear what I hear?
1985

Buenos días and *hasta luego*
in boardrooms and strategy sessions.
Where are your grateful holiday smiles,
bilinguals? I've given you a voice,
let you in
to hear old friends tell old jokes.
Stop flinching. Drink egg nog. Hum along.

> Not carols we hear
> whimpering
> children too cold
> to sing
> on Christmas eve.

Do you see what I see

adding a dash of color
to conferences and corporate parties
one per panel or office
slight south-of-the-border seasoning
feliz navidad and *próspero año nuevo*, right?
Relax. Eat rum balls. Watch the snow.

> No twinkling lights
> we see but
> searchlights
> seeking illegal aliens
> outside our thick windows.

To change focus, here's a more celebratory poem by Li-Young Lee. Pay attention to the line breaks, the use of words that begin with "b," "p," and "d," which themselves are close in sound; then try to feel the rhythm and melody they set up:

From Blossoms
From blossoms comes
this brown paper bag of peaches
we bought from the boy
at the bend in the road where we turned toward
signs painted *Peaches.*

From laden boughs, from hands,
from sweet fellowship in the bins,
comes nectar at the roadside, succulent
peaches we devour, dusty skin and all,
comes the familiar dust of summer, dust we eat.

O, to take what we love inside,
to carry within us an orchard, to eat
not only the skin, but the shade,
not only the sugar, but the days, to hold
the fruit in our hands, adore it, then bite into
the round jubilance of peach.

There are days we live
as if death were nowhere
in the background, from joy
to joy to joy, from wing to wing,
from blossom to blossom to
impossible blossom, to sweet impossible blossom.

The six words beginning with "b" in the first four lines (*blossoms, brown, bag, bought, boy, bend*) are not accidental but poetic choices. The blossoms in the bag bought from the boy set up a soft melody. This is not a hostile poem but a love poem, in the largest sense of love for the world and its multiple tastes, sounds, and smells.

The last three lines illustrate the way in which repetitions of words and sounds build the melody and rhythm of a poem: there is "from joy / to joy to joy," "wing" to "wing," and four "blossoms'" bringing the poem back to the "b's" that also are buzzing around the blossoms, carrying off the pollen and fertilizing other crops and creating sweet honey.

Of course, you don't have to analyze this poem in a complex way to love it. But it helps to think about the way words echo each other; sounds repeat to create a mood, tone, and melody for the whole; and spacing provides a score for reading the whole.

My preference in reading a poem is to analyze it enough to feel comfortable reading the text. I don't go deep into the structure in the way a poet or critic does. I'm a reader in the way I'm a listener of music. My son, a composer, looks at a piece of music from an analytical as well as an emotional way. He reads scores, takes apart the harmonies and dissonances. He has a professional interest in the making of music, whereas my interest is in being an informed listener. The hints in this chapter are meant for an informed reader of poems, not a working poet or a professional critic.

I came across an interesting example of the difference between these ways of approaching poetry in a commentary W. D. Snodgrass wrote on this poem of his:

W. D. Snodgrass:
Owls
—for Camille
 Wait; the great horned owls
Calling from the wood's edge; listen.
There: the dark male, low
And booming, tremoring the whole valley.
There: the female, resolving, answering
High and clear, restoring silence.
The chilly woods draw in
Their breath, slow, waiting, and now both
Sound out together, close to harmony.

These are the year's worst nights.
Ice glazed on the top boughs,
Old snow deep on the ground,
Snow in the red-tailed hawks'
Nests they take for their own.
Nothing crosses the crusted ground.
No squirrels, no rabbits, the mice gone,
No crow has young yet they can steal.
These nights the iron air clangs
Like the gates of a cell block, blank
And black as the inside of your chest.

Now, the great owls take
The air, the male's calls take
Depth on and resonance, they take
A rough nest, take their mate
And, opening out long wings, take
Flight, unguided and apart, to caliper
The blind synapse their voices cross
Over the dead white fields,
The dead black woods, where they take
Soundings on nothing fast, take
Soundings on each other, each alone.

For my own poem, I took for my theme-rhythm the
call of the Great Horned Owl:

HOó, hoo-Hóo, Hóo, Hóo.

My first line reproduces that rhythm closely:

Wait, the Great Hor'ned Owls,/

The second line adds to this basic four-beat rhythm
several unaccented syllables:

Cálling from the woóds' edge, lísten. /

The third drops the extra syllable, repeating the basic pattern:

There: the dark mále, lów /

but immediately rushes into the fourth line, where many more unaccented syllables are added:

And bóoming, tremoring the whóle válley.

And so on throughout the poem; when such a technique works well, I think it will seem not only a restraint, a limit on the poem's energies, but will come to be identified with that energy itself, an energy which is only strengthened by being re-strained and channelled.

Naturally, I don't expect readers to know of this theme-and-variations structure, much less know that this theme is the rhythm of the owl's call. We don't usually ask about the principles of construction in a building we like; we just use it that much more. Now I must abide the test of seeing how many people will want to inhabit and use my structure and for how long.

I believe the last line of Snodgrass's commentary is worth repeating: "Now I must abide the test of seeing how many people will want to inhabit and use my structure and for how long." The reader is the tester he refers to. It is us, the readers, who make the poem heard or keep it inert in unread books. The complex infrastructure of many poems is wonderful to study but not necessary to understand in order to read and love a poem. One does not have to understand the way a poem is made in order to be a sophisticated and knowledgeable reader of the poem. You don't have to know harmonic theory or the complexity of jazz chord structures to know and love jazz, and you don't have to be an expert on syntax and grammar to appreciate a good essay or novel. The same is true for a poem. You can develop an informed habit of reading poems without having to be a structural critic or academic student of poetry.

Here's a poem, "Delta" by Adrienne Rich, which you've already encountered in the Introduction. Read it again and try to get a sense of the melody Rich is playing:

> ### Delta
> If you have taken this rubble for my past
> raking through it for fragments you could sell
> know that I long ago moved on
> deeper into the heart of the matter
>
> If you think you can grasp me, think again;
> my story flows in more than one direction
> a delta springing from the riverbed
> with its five fingers spread

The poem begins with a supposition: "If you have taken . . ." and the poet replies, "know that I long ago moved on / deeper into the heart of the matter." The tempo picks up and "my story flows in more than one direction." In fact, it flows like water running into a delta.

It's not clear whom the poet is addressing. It could be a critic who feels he or she has got her fixed for once and all time as a poet, or a publisher or editor, "raking through it for fragments you could sell." It could be a former lover. It could be the reader.

The rhythm and melody of the poem move like water down to the delta, which flows off into many streams. It speaks to the poet's complexity and personal growth, to the inability to capture a living working poet in past poems. The line breaks lead the reader, though the image of water flowing through the delta emerges only in the second stanza. Read the poem out loud and visualize flowing water. And think of the last image, which is not of a delta but of a human hand

with its five fingers spread. The poet is growing and will not be tied
to her past or captured by other people's assessment of work she has
already done. She is flowing out in many directions.

Here's a very different poem, but one that also uses flowing
water as an image, by William Stafford. Read it and, in this case,
pay attention not merely to the line breaks and sounds, but to the
adjectives and adverbs and the way in which they intensify the
poem's impression.

> ### In Hurricane Canyon
> After we talked, after the moon
> rose, before we went to bed, we
> sat quietly. That was when
> we heard the river, big stones
> bumping along the bottom from
> away up the mountain.
>
> How terribly shredded and lonely
> the water went as it cried out and
> held splinters of moonlight, and its
> life raced powerfully on! That night,
> we bowed, shadowed our eyes,
> and followed—all the way down—
> one, slow, helpless, bumping stone.

In line four, there are "big stones," which makes all the differ-
ence. Big stones bumping along the bottom of a river are not the
same as stones bumping along it. The water is shredded and
lonely, held splinters of the moon, and the sense of the power of
the water and the smallness of the people is magnified. These
modifiers shape the melody as well, providing color and shade to
the poet's portrait. Paying specific attention to the details a poet
chooses to include is another way to enter closer into the poem.

In the case of this poem by Derek Walcott, there is a dialogue
between the poet and his double in the mirror. As you read this
poem, which is denser and requires more effort than the Stafford

poem, you have to, as they say in music, play the breaks, attend to
the sounds, listen for the tone and melody expressed in the modi-
fiers, and at the same time keep the poet's voice and meaning in
mind. This sounds like a formidable task, but good poetry coheres
and all of these elements come together. Sometimes an effort or
analysis is necessary; sometimes the poem speaks directly to you.
Every poem does not have to be analyzed, but some poems require
it. It's your choice as to the kind of reader you want to be and the
effort you choose to put forth to make poetry a part of your life. It's
the same thing with music—some people wonder how songs are
composed, others want to read the scores and play them. Yet others
want to compose their own music and learn from other composers'
work, and most people just want to listen to the music. All these
ways of relating to music and poetry make sense to me. Readers
don't need to be poets or critics, although of course we can choose
to experiment with criticism or writing poems.

XI

My double, tired of morning, closes the door
of the motel bathroom; then, wiping the steamed mirror,
refuses to acknowledge me staring back at him.
With the softest grunt, he stretches my throat for the function
of scraping it clean, his dispassionate care
like a barber's lathering a corpse—extreme unction.
The old ritual would have been as grim
if the small wisps that curled there in the basin
were not hairs but minuscular seraphim.
He clips our moustache with a snickering scissors,
then stops, reflecting, midair. Certain sadnesses
are not immense, but fatal, like the sense of sin
while shaving. And empty cupboards where her dresses
shone. But why flushing a faucet, its vortex
swivelling with bits of hair, could make some men's
hands quietly put aside their razors,
and sense their veins as filth floating downriver
after the dolorous industries of sex,
is a question swans may raise with their white necks,
that the cockerel answers quickly, treading his hens.

The poet places himself in the mirror watching his double, and from that distance describes his double shaving their collective face. The double is tired, grunts, stretches the poet's throat and scrapes it and then lathers it as though it was a corpse. The scissors snicker; the language is harsh and then sad. The poem ends with the image of the cockerel stomping on his hens. This is an anti-love story condensed into an episode of shaving. The language of the poem is harsh, dissonant, deliberately not graceful, and I feel that its melody is much closer to a piece of contemporary music that has a single harsh discordant line. It is anti-tuneful. Reading it this way, taking hints from the words and the breaks, I find it powerfully speaking to the emptiness and self-loathing one can feel after having destroyed a relationship.

4

The Images at the Heart of Poems

Not to Have . . .
Not to have but to be.
The black heart of the poppy,
O to lie there as seed.
To become the beloved.
As the world ends, to enter
the last note of its music.

There are a number of ways to look at the language of poetry. In poetry classes the study of what are called tropes, such as metaphor, metonymy, and synecdoche, is very useful for the analysis of poetry. But I have found that in introducing new readers to contemporary poetry it is more helpful to focus on what could be called the central images in a poem. This helps develop the habit of reading poems rather than analyzing them. I don't want to marginalize the importance of analyzing the structure and nature of poems nor the complex critical task of sorting out poetic genres, judging excellence, and uncovering trends and techniques. But what I do hope this book and this way of looking at poems can do is develop the habit of reading first and not having analysis get in the way of the development of a taste for poetry.

As a first example of the image at the heart of a poem, consider Denise Levertov's "Not to Have...." The central image is the "black heart of a poppy," and to feel the poem it is important to visualize a poppy and figure out what that black heart might be. Levertov, like many poets, looks closely at particulars as she crafts her work.

What does the black heart of a poppy look like? How is it constructed? I actually found a dying poppy on a roadside near my house and looked at it very carefully after reading this short poem for the first time. There were black seeds at the center, the potential for new birth, the hope to keep this beauty alive in the world. But the same poppy seeds also produce opium and are therefore dangerous, seductive, intoxicating. The image at the center of this short poem is visual and sensual and prepares the reader for the second stanza, which moves directly from the seed to being the beloved, the generator of the seed, and then, by what a filmmaker would call a jump cut, to ecstasy and the end of the world. To be the beloved at the final moment at the end of the world or at the end of one's life, to be loved until the very last moment of the very last sound of the final Requiem (I hear Mozart's *Requiem* here, but each reader will hear her or his own music), may be the best we finite beings can experience.

I found myself compelled to copy this short poem centered on the image of the heart of a poppy and put it up in my study—to make it part of my life until the wall becomes so full of new poems that it is covered up by other images and other sentiments.

Visualization is integral to the reading of poetry. It is important to sense and feel and even see, taste, hear, almost touch the central images and let the poet's words work with these images in your mind.

Here's a short poem from the Introduction to this book, Rita Dove's "Canary." It's worth reading it again and pausing to reflect on the title before plunging into the poem. When I think of a canary I think of a beautiful songster confined in a cage, of a bird that probably couldn't survive outside of cage in an urban environment. Even though a canary never appears in the poem, the title provides an image that haunts it.

Canary
for Michael S. Harper
Billie Holiday's burned voice
had as many shadows as lights,
a mournful candelabra against a sleek piano,
the gardenia her signature under that ruined face.

(Now you're cooking, drummer to bass,
magic spoon, magic needle.
Take all day if you have to
with your mirror and your bracelet of song.)

Fact is, the invention of women under siege
has been to sharpen love in the service of myth.

If you can't be free, be a mystery.

The poem is a tribute to the tragic and caged life of the blues
and jazz singer Billie Holiday, ending with the bittersweet "If you
can't be free, be a mystery." It is also about all women "under
siege." The image of the caged bird does not prepare the reader for
the particular nature or language of the poem, or for the way in
which the poet relates to her subject. But I find that it helps frame
the whole, and that while reading the poem I keep an image of the
bird and its song and of Billie Holiday and her voice playing back
and forth in my imagination, giving the poem a sound and density
that make it memorable. This complex interplay of image and lan-
guage heightens attention, not just to the poem itself, but to caged
women and manufactured love.

There are different, more ironic and wilder images at the cen-
ter of some poems. For example, consider the hurricane at the cen-
ter of this poem by Victor Hernández Cruz. Before reading the
poem, imagine being in the midst of a hurricane, seeing objects
and maybe even people blown about by uncontrollable winds, feel-
ing the water and wild air rushing down your street and through
your house. This visualization helps let the poet take you over and

in this case take you by surprise at what the poet does with the winds and the flying objects.

> *Problems with Hurricanes*
> A campesino looked at the air
> And told me:
> With hurricanes it's not the wind
> or the noise or the water.
> I'll tell you he said:
> it's the mangoes, avocados
> Green plantains and bananas
> flying into town like projectiles.
>
> How would your family
> feel if they had to tell
> The generations that you
> got killed by a flying
> Banana.
>
> Death by drowning has honor
> If the wind picked you up
> and slammed you
> Against a mountain boulder
> This would not carry shame
> But
> to suffer a mango smashing
> Your skull
> or a plantain hitting your
> Temple at 70 miles per hour
> is the ultimate disgrace.
>
> The campesino takes off his hat—
> As a sign of respect
> towards the fury of the wind
> And says:
> Don't worry about the noise
> Don't worry about the water
> Don't worry about the wind—

If you are going out
beware of mangoes
And all such beautiful
sweet things.

The poem is about the tropics, about honor, and dignity, and about "all such beautiful things." Using the hurricane image, Hernández Cruz provides a hilarious mix of flying fruit, death, pride, and future generations that cannot be paraphrased in prose, reduced to a weather report, or even represented on video. Like all good poems, "Problems with Hurricanes" has a quality that is not reducible to any paraphrase. It stands as a poetic flight of the imagination that is delightful for its own sake, and an ironic challenge to rethink natural disasters as social embarrassments.

Sometimes the central image in a poem refers to some literary work or event or character outside the poem. In order to enter the world of the poem you have to become familiar with that external reference, and so every once in a while reading poetry demands that the reader do some research. Fortunately, if the poem is wonderful, the time spent on the research is more than rewarded by the experience provided by the poem. Even if it isn't, the research might provide some interesting learning in and of itself.

"Jacob's Ladder" by Denise Levertov is a poem I have read and reread over the years. When I first approached the poem, it occurred to me that I didn't really know the specific biblical reference to Jacob's ladder, although knowing Levertov's work there was no question that she knew, had read, and most likely memorized the specific passage that refers to it.

Since there are so many biblical references in poetry and literature in general, and since I am not fluent in the Bible, I've found and use a wonderful reference book that helps me navigate the Old and New Testaments. It is a paperback entitled *Cruden's Handy Concordance to the Bible* (published by Lamplighter Books, Zondervan Publishing House, Grand Rapids, MI). The *Concordance* is arranged as a dictionary and lists every name, place, and subject covered in the Bible. You can find listings such as "pride," "repentance," "vomit," "fire," and so forth. It took me a second to look up Jacob and discover that Jacob's ladder appears in Genesis 28. Since the references in the *Concordance* are to chapter and verse, any Bible you own can be used to find the relevant text.

In the *New Oxford Annotated Bible* Jacob's dream, in which he saw the ladder, is translated in the following way:

> And he dreamed that there was a ladder set up on the earth, and the top of it reached to heaven; and behold, the Angels of God were ascending and descending on it. And the Lord stood above it and said, "I am the Lord, the God of Abraham your father and the God of Isaac; the land on which you lie I will give to you and your descendants; and your descendants shall be like the dust of the earth, and you shall spread abroad to the west and to the east and to the north and to the south; and by you and your descendants shall all the families of the earth bless themselves. Behold, I am with you and will keep you wherever you go, and will bring you back to this land; for I will not leave you until I have done that of which I have spoken to you." Then Jacob awoke from his sleep and said, "Surely the Lord is in this place; and I did not know it." And he was afraid, and he said, "How awesome is this place! This is none other than the house of God, and this is the gate of heaven."

After reading this, try Denise Levertov's poem.

Jacob's Ladder
The stairway is not
a thing of gleaming strands
a radiant evanescence
for angels' feet that only glance in their
tread, and need not
touch the stone.

It is of stone.
A rosy stone that takes
a glowing tone of softness
only because behind it the sky is a doubtful,
a doubting
night gray.

A stairway of sharp
angles, solidly built.
One sees that the angels must spring
down from one step to the next, giving
a little
lift of the wings:

and a man climbing
must scrape his knees, and bring
the grip of his hands into play. The cut stone
consoles his groping feet. Wings brush past
him.
The poem ascends.

Levertov's "Jacob's Ladder" is not made of gold or marble and
is not easy to ascend or descend. The angels have to make an effort
to descend, and people have to climb up, often getting a bit blood-
ied in the process. The gate of heaven, in the imagination of the
poet, is transformed into a pathway on which angels and people
touch gently and on which the poem itself ascends with and is like
the people, struggling but touched by an angel.

The power of Levertov's poem is dependent upon the power of
Jacob's dream. One text influences and enhances the other. This is
often the case with poetry. Poets do not write in a vacuum. They
write from their experiences and perceptions, but those experi-
ences and perceptions are with other poetry and literature as well as
with the world. As a reader of poetry, I have begun to see that the
wonderful relationships among poems and the way in which poets
use other poetic texts or references to historical, mythic, or literary
sources is an enhancement of their own work, not an undue influ-

ence or borrowing. It's the same with music, which builds upon and enriches its past as new forms emerge.

Here's another angel poem, by Robert Hass. The perspective is thoroughly different, as is the central image. The angels are looking down at lovers, at humanity, at the beauty created by mortality and fallibility. This image of angels looking down from heaven at a couple making love is central to the poem's ability to celebrate the finiteness and privilege of being. It is the angels here who are illiterate, in the complex ways of human beings who are subject to dying.

Privilege of Being

Many are making love. Up above, the angels
in the unshaken ether and crystal of human longing
are braiding one another's hair, which is strawberry
blond
and the texture of cold rivers. They glance
down from time to time at the awkward ecstasy—
it must look to them like featherless birds
splashing in the spring puddle of a bed—
and then one woman, she is about to come,
peels back the man's shut eyelids and says,
look at me, and he does. Or is it the man
tugging the curtain rope in that dark theater?
Anyway, they do, they look at each other;
two beings with evolved eyes, rapacious,
startled, connected at the belly in an unbelievably
sweet
lubricious glue, stare at each other,
and the angels are desolate. They hate it. They
shudder pathetically
like lithographs of Victorian beggars
with perfect features and alabaster skin hawking rags
in the lewd alleys of the novel.

All of creation is offended by this distress.
It is like the keening sound the moon makes
sometimes,
rising. The lovers especially cannot bear it,
it fills them with unspeakable sadness, so that
they close their eyes again and hold each other,
each feeling the mortal singularity of the body
they have enchanted out of death for an hour or so,
and one day, running at sunset, the woman says to the
man,
*I woke up feeling so sad this morning because I
realized*
that you could not, as much as I love you,
dear heart, cure my loneliness,
wherewith she touched his cheek to reassure him
that she did not mean to hurt him with this truth.
And the man is not hurt exactly,
he understands that life has limits, that people
die young, fail at love,
fail of their ambitions. He runs beside her, he thinks
of the sadness they have gasped and crooned their
way out of
coming, clutching each other with old, invented
forms of grace and clumsy gratitude, ready
to be alone again, or dissatisfied, or merely
companionable like the couples on the summer beach
reading magazine articles about intimacy between the
sexes
to themselves, and to each other,
and to the immense, illiterate, consoling angels.

And here's a third, very different angel poem by Carolyn Forché, "The Recording Angel." After a bit of research I found specific references in the Bible to the Book of Life, in which a recording angel has written down the deeds of people on earth. In Revelation 20:12 there is a description of the use of these entries in the Book of Life:

> And I saw the dead, great and small, standing before
> the throne, and books were opened. Also another
> book was opened which is the Book of Life. And the
> dead were judged by what was written in the book,
> by what they had done. And the sea gave up the
> dead in it, Death and Hades gave up the dead in
> them, all were judged by what they had done.

I do not know whether Carolyn Forché had this particular passage
in mind when she wrote this poem, but she certainly had the *Book of
Life* and the Day of Judgment in her consciousness. This is not an easy
poem and requires several readings. The meanings of images and
events in the beginning are clarified at the end. But the central image of
the recording angel (who is that angel in the poem) ties things together
and makes the coherence of the whole comprehensible and, for me,
moving and upsetting. I found that I had to read this poem more than
once to have it make sense. On a third reading I felt that I could enter
into the painful experience the poet was portraying and think about the
moral decisions we all have to make when we encounter the terrible.

The Recording Angel

Memory insists she stood there, able to go neither forward nor back,
and in that Unanimous night, time slowed, in light pulsing
through ash, light of which the coat was
    made
Light of their brick houses
In matter's choreography of light, time slowed, then reversed until
memory
Held her, able to go neither forward nor back
They were alone where once hundreds of thousands lived

Doves, or rather their wings, heard above the roof and the linens floating
Above a comic wedding in which corpses exchange vows. A grand funeral celebration Everyone has died at once
Walking home always, always on this same blue road, cold through the black-and-white
    trees
Unless the film were reversed, she wouldn't reach the house
As she doesn't in her memory, or in her dream
Often she hears him calling out, half her name, his own, behind her in a room until she
    turns
Standing forever, where often she hears him calling out

He is there, hidden in the blue winter fields and the burnt acreage of summer
As if, in reflecting the ruins, the river were filming what their city had been
And *had it not been for this* lines up behind *if it weren't for that*
Until the past is something of a regiment
Yet looking back down the row of marching faces one sees one face
Before the shelling, these balconies were for geraniums and children
The slate roofs for morning

Market flowers in a jar, a string of tied garlic, and a voice moving off as if fearing itself
Under the leprous trees a white siren of light searches
Under the leprous trees a white siren of sun

II

A row of cabanas with white towels near restorative waters where once it was possible
    to be cured
A town of vacant summer houses
Mists burning the slightest lapse of sea
The child has gone to the window filled with desire, a glass light passing through its hand
There are tide tables by which the sea had been predictable, as were the heavens
As sickness chose from among us we grew fewer
There were jetty lights where there was no jetty
What the rain forests had been became our difficult breath

At the moment when the snow geese lifted, thousands at once after days of crying in
    the wetlands
At once they lifted in a single ascent, acres of wind in their wingbones
Wetlands of morning light in their lift moving as one over the continent
As a white front, one in their radiance, in their crying, a cloud of one desire

The child plays with its dead telephone. The father blows a kiss. The child laughs
The fire of his few years is carried toward the child on a cake
The child can't help itself. Would each day be like this?

And the geese, rising and falling in the rain on a surf of black hands
Sheets of rain and geese invisible or gone

Someone was supposed to have come
Waves turning black with the beach weed called dead men's hands
The sea strikes a bottle against a rock

III

The photographs were found at first by mistake in the drawer. After
that I went to
    them often
She was standing on her toes in a silk *yukata*, her arms raised
Wearing a girl's white socks and near her feet a vase of calla lilies
Otherwise she wore nothing
And in this one, her long hair is gathered into a white towel
Or tied back not to interfere
She had been wounded by so many men, abused by them
From behind in a silk *yukata*, then like this
One morning they were gone and I searched his belongings for them
like a madwoman
In every direction, melted railyards, felled telegraph poles
For two months to find some trace of her
Footsteps on the floor above. More birds
It might have been less painful had it not been for the photographs
And beyond the paper walls, the red maple
Shirt in the wind of what the past meant
The fresh claw of a swastika on Rue Boulard
A man walking until he can no longer be seen
Don't say I was there. Always say I was never there.

Here's a poem by Martin Espada that also has biblical resonances.
Before reading the poem, think of the title, which also introduces
the central image: "Trumpets from the Islands of Their Eviction."
Trumpets sounding—what kind of trumpets? Music from the past,
trumpets announcing an important event, trumpets muted or blaring?
Trumpets sounding from islands where people have been evicted, com-
ing to them where they are now? A little thought given to this title (not
every poet helps the reader with a title) provides a way into the poem.

I've always found that such hints help me think my way into a
first reading of a poem, especially a complex one that I know I
won't get, much less love, the first time around.

Trumpets from the Islands of Their Eviction

At the bar two blocks away,
immigrants with Spanish mouths
hear trumpets
from the islands of their eviction.
The music swarms into the barrio
of a refugee's imagination,
along with predatory squad cars
and bullying handcuffs.

Their eviction:
like Mrs. Alfaro, evicted
when she trapped ten mice,
sealed them in plastic sandwich bags
and gifted them to the landlord;
like Daniel, the boy stockaded
in the back of retarded classrooms
for having no English
to comfort third-grade teachers;
like my father thirty-five years ago,
brown skin darker than the Air Force uniform
that could not save him, seven days countyjailed
for refusing the back of a Mississippi bus;
like the nameless Florida jibaro
the grocery stores would not feed
in spite of the dollars he showed,
who returned with a machete,
collected cans from shelves
and forced the money
into the clerk's reluctant staring hand.

We are the ones identified by case number,
summons in the wrong language,
judgment without stay of execution.
Mrs. Alfaro has thirty days
to bundle the confusion of five children
down claustrophobic stairs
and away from the apartment.

And at the bar two blocks away,
immigrants with Spanish mouths
hear trumpets
from the islands of their eviction.
The sound scares away devils
like tropical fish
darting between the corals.

The poem begins and ends in a bar with Spanish immigrants hearing the trumpets. These stanzas frame a litany of the immigrant experience that ranges from the eviction of someone in the neighborhood to the racist treatment of the poet's father. This litany is like a bill of particulars, not whining or crying but stating what needs redress using specific examples, not abstract arguments. This makes the poem both visceral and political.

The middle stanzas read like concrete versions of those parts of the Declaration of Independence where England's abuses are listed to justify a call to action. And here the trumpets come in again, but they are coming from the islands people have had to flee, not from the mainland. Those trumpets scare away devils—what kind of warning or exorcism is the poet talking about? What is sounding out over the sea that is coming here to create justice? The poem, in a condensed and moving way, talks about what people bring here with them and what connects them to the places of their origins, and also implies that redemption may come from these places of origin, not from the U.S.

In this poem by Jane Hirshfield the central image has to be extracted from the poem itself. Read it through and try to identify and then visualize the overriding poetic image that the author puts at the center of the poem.

The New Silence
There are times
when the heart closes down,
the metal grate drawn
and padlocked,
the owner's footprints covered by snow.

Someone may come to peer through the glass,
but soon leaves.
Someone may come to clean, but turns away.

What is still inside
settles down for the darkness: clocks stop,
newspapers pass out of date.

The new silence goes unheard
under so many grindings of engines,
so many sounds of construction.

Only the three pigeons,
refusing to eat,
lower their heads and grieve.

On the surface this poem's central image is that of a closed and abandoned house. But the poem is not just the image, for it is as much about the heart and the self (as the first two lines make clear) as about a house. Poetic images have density–they are and are not just themselves. Often they merge aspects of the physical world with thought, feeling, and history in condensed and intense ways. Once the multiple meanings of a poem become apparent, reading itself becomes a different activity. It is not a matter of searching for a meaning so much as of letting the many meanings embodied in the same words reveal themselves.

I do not feel comfortable with the mystical-sounding language that I find necessary to use when describing the difference between reading poetry and prose. But there is a sense of open reading, of not looking for a linear tale or single point or simple summary, that is essential for mining the pleasures and sometimes challenging confrontations that poetry can provoke. To read a poem is to relax one's sense of the ordinary, to let things that don't obviously go together merge, to entertain multiple meanings without privileging one, and to make oneself vulnerable to new language, new images, and new ways of stretching the imagination.

Here's another example of a poetic encounter with multiple meanings. The title of Robert Duncan's poem "Often I Am Permitted to Return to a Meadow," which is also its first line, provides hints to the nature of the poem and the poet's attitude within his narrative.

In this poem the "I" tells the reader that the poet is within the poem and has been within the meadow. It's worth thinking about the title before plunging into the poem.

Here is a free association on that line, not a unique one but one that helped me enter into the poem:

> Often, but not always, I am permitted (who controls the permissions?) to return—when and why and how has the poet been there before, to a meadow—why a meadow, think about and visualize the meadows I have seen and those I have returned to and those I want to return to and those that I am, for one reason or another, not permitted to return to—perhaps because they no longer exist or because I have moved to a different place and left a place I love and am not likely to return to.

There are no answers to the questions, but images and ideas that open me up to Duncan's perceptions, ideas, and exceptional language.

> ***Often I Am Permitted to Return to a Meadow***
> as if it were a scene made-up by the mind,
> that is not mine, but is a made place,
>
> that is mine, it is so near to the heart,
> an eternal pasture folded in all thought
> so that there is a hall therein
>
> that is a made place, created by light
> wherefrom the shadows that are forms fall.

Wherefrom fall all architectures I am
I say are likenesses of the First Beloved
whose flowers are flames lit to the Lady.

She it is Queen Under The Hill
whose hosts are a disturbance of words within words
that is a field folded.

It is only a dream of the grass blowing
east against the source of the sun
in an hour before the sun's going down

whose secret we see in a children's game
of ring a round of roses told.

Often I am permitted to return to a meadow
as if it were a given property of the mind
that certain bounds hold against chaos,

that is a place of first permission,
everlasting omen of what is.

This is what I call a slow-reading poem. Duncan weighs every idea and image and moves slowly through thought and feeling to recollection, metaphysics, and religion. There is no separating all of these complex interactions. The central image of a meadow—a real meadow and one that is a "made-place" and an "eternal pasture," "a field folded," a "dream of the grass blowing / east against the source of the sun," "a place of first permission, / everlasting omen of what is"—is one that has invaded my dreams.

I love this poem and am not sure why. I feel the same secret, allusive sense of a special place where I can and can't go, and have images of an imaginary place that provides "bounds . . . against chaos."

Robert Duncan's poetry has always been a puzzlement and a challenge to me–I don't understand everything in the poems, and that's why I love them so much and continue to read and reread them. Poetry is not once and for all, and when one encounters a poet like Duncan whose images, meaning, and sensibility are complex and often very personal, the best thing to do is honor and read and reread them and then decide whether you care for their work. Give poets a chance, but be clear that ultimately you are the judge of the meaning of poetry for you. Don't pretend to like poems simply because you think you should.

Poets themselves often don't see everything in the poems they write. Often the creative act itself brings forth unanticipated meanings and nuances, and the work transcends anything intended or felt by the poet. There's a story told by E. Martin Browne, the director of all of T. S. Eliot's plays. Evidently at a cocktail party shortly after the opening of his play *The Cocktail Party* Eliot was besieged by a woman who had just seen the play and proceeded to tell the author in some detail about the play's symbolism and what it meant.

Eliot listened intently to her analysis and when she was done said, "You know, you may be right. You may be right."

This was not meant as a put-down so much as an acknowledgment that it is not surprising and is in fact quite wonderful that there is more in a work of art than even the artist knows or can understand.

Joy Harjo's work derives from her experience as a woman, a Native American, and a person trying to thrive in a complex and often hostile world. This poem is rooted in these experiences, but since its central image is release of fear, it is also a poetic and imaginative representation of what many of us have experienced as we make decisions to be ourselves and not live in the fear of the oppression our families have experienced on cultural or personal levels. I find it easy to relate to on a personal level even though I am not female and not Native American. Nor do I feel I have to experience the poem in the same way that a woman or a Native American would experience it, although I can certainly project myself into the minds of other readers. Nevertheless, the poem can be meaningful for me in terms of my own experiences and concerns.

I find this modest attitude very helpful when encountering voices from cultures and perspectives I cannot fully participate in. Instead of closing myself off from the multitude of voices now speaking out in American poetry, I can enter into many unfamiliar worlds and try to orient myself within them in terms of my own human concerns and pains and fears and pleasures. It's been very rewarding. For example, I don't have to completely understand or identify with what Joy Harjo writes for her poems to make my life richer and broaden my understanding, not merely of her culture and perspective, but of life in general.

The central image Harjo's poem "I Give You Back" is not of a place or a person but of a complex psychological decision that profoundly affects one's life—giving back debts and profits of a complex relationship.

I Give You Back
I release you, my beautiful and terrible
fear. I release you. You were my beloved
and hated twin, but now, I don't know you
as myself. I release you with all the
pain I would know at the death of
my daughters.

You are not my blood anymore.

I give you back to the white soldiers
who burned down my home, beheaded my children,
raped and sodomized my brothers and sisters.
I give you back to those who stole the
food from our plates when we were starving.

I release you, fear, because you hold
these scenes in front of me and I was born
with eyes that can never close.

I release you, fear, so you can no longer
keep me naked and frozen in the winter,
or smothered under blankets in the summer.

I release you
I release you
I release you
I release you

I am not afraid to be angry.
I am not afraid to rejoice.
I am not afraid to be black.
I am not afraid to be white.
I am not afraid to be hungry.
I am not afraid to be full.
I am not afraid to be hated.
I am not afraid to be loved,
to be loved, to be loved, fear.

Oh, you have choked me, but I gave you the leash.
You have gutted me, but I gave you the knife.
You have devoured me, but I laid myself across the fire.
You held my mother down and raped her,
        but I gave you the heated thing.

I take myself back, fear.
You are not my shadow any longer.
I won't hold you in my hands.
You can't live in my eyes, my ears, my voice
my belly, or in my heart my heart
my heart   my heart

But come here, fear
I am alive and you are so afraid
           of dying.

There are ghosts at the center of poems as well as feelings,
places, and living people. Here are two poems, the first by Robert

Bly and the second by Li-Young Lee, where the ghost or memory
of a dead father frames the poem and becomes the central image
that leads the poet to talk about experience, love, regret, and liv-
ing within the world with the spirit and memory of the dead. In
one case the dead father calls out, in the other he is reading out
loud in heaven.

When My Dead Father Called

Last night I dreamt my father called to us.
He was stuck somewhere. It took us
A long time to dress, I don't know why.
The night was snowy; there were long black roads.

Finally, we reached the little town, Bellingham.
There he stood, by a streetlamp in cold wind,
Snow blowing along the sidewalk. I noticed
The uneven sort of shoes that men wore

In the early Forties. And overalls. He was smoking.
Why did it take us so long to get going? Perhaps
He left us somewhere once, or did I simply
Forget he was alone in winter in some town?

My Father, in Heaven, Is Reading Out Loud

My father, in heaven, is reading out loud
to himself Psalms or news. Now he ponders what
he's read. No. He is listening for the sound
of children in the yard. Was that laughing
or crying? So much depends upon the
answer, for either he will go on reading,
or he'll run to save a child's day from grief.
As it is in heaven, so it was on earth.

Because my father walked the earth with a grave,
determined rhythm, my shoulders ached
from his gaze. Because my father's shoulders
ached from the pulling of oars, my life now moves
with a powerful back-and-forth rhythm:
nostalgia, speculation. Because he
made me recite a book a month, I forget
everything as soon as I read it. And knowledge
never comes but while I'm mid-stride a flight
of stairs, or lost a moment on some avenue.

A remarkable disappointment to him,
I am like anyone who arrives late
in the millennium and is unable
to stay to the end of days. The world's
beginnings are obscure to me, its outcomes
inaccessible. I don't understand
the source of starlight, or starlight's destinations.
And already another year slides out
of balance. But I don't disparage scholars;
my father was one and I loved him,
who packed his books once, and all of our belongings,
then sat down to await instruction
from his god, yes, but also from a radio.
At the doorway, I watched, and I suddenly
knew he was one like me, who got my learning
under a lintel; he was one of the powerless,
to whom knowledge came while he sat among
suitcases, boxes, old newspapers, string.

He did not decide peace or war, home or exile,
escape by land or escape by sea.
He waited merely, as always someone
waits, far, near, here, hereafter, to find out:
is it praise or lament hidden in the next moment?

In "You Are Real as Earth, y Más" by Ana Castillo, the title gives the reader insight into the central image of the poem. The question, however, is, what is "real earth"? And for those who don't know a bit of Spanish, it is essential to know that "*y Más*" means "and more." You are more real than real earth. It is interesting that the English word "real" with the same spelling means *royal* in Spanish. I'm sure the poet knows this, so the implication of the title is that the "you" being addressed is as royal as earth.

Earth is not dirt. It is the fertile soil that produces food, sustains people, gives rise to flavors and tastes—to the chile ristra in the first line, the hot pepper, the salsa of life. You don't need to have tasted a chile ristra to know the sting, bite, and joy Castillo is referring to, but it doesn't hurt to have had hot sauce a few times.

The image of real earth helps understand the intensity and passion of the poem. The word "real" is not used like it's used in the phrase "it's real cool"—it has a different intensity, rooted in the experience of people who work the soil and revere it.

You Are Real as Earth, y Más
1990
I
A green chile ristra
you are, 'manito——
hung upside down,
on a rustic porch.

Rock, you are,
coyote, roadrunner,
scorpion stung
still running strong. Sometimes,
you are a red ristra
into whom I take burning bites
and always yearn for one
more
bite.
You are real as earth, y más.
You are air and sky. While I—
who have traveled so far to reach you,
remain the blood of fertility,
fear of your mortality,
pungent waters in which
you believe, you will surely
die a godless death.

II
And when you are not sky,
nor warm rain,
nor dust or a pebble in my shoe,
you are the smoke
of an old curandera's cigar
trailing throughout my rooms.
You are the Warrior Monkey
in a Chinese Buddhist tale; you are
copper and gold filigree—
Tlaquepaque glass blown
into the vague shape of a man,
a jaguar, a gnat. I
look for signs to see if it is really you.
Tonantzín appears as Guadalupe
on a burnt tortilla.

Coffee grounds, wax, an egg dropped
into a clear jar of water.
I look for signs everywhere.

III
I have lit farolitos to guide
you back to my door.
Turned upside down by desire,
it seems your feet
are on a groundless path. Beware of the Trickster.
The road in either direction
is neither longer nor shorter,
nor more narrow nor wider
than the fear that closes your heart.
Grey ash sediment in my entrails,
this path of ours is Sacred Ground.

There are many references in this poem that many readers
might not be familiar with: Tlaquepaque, curandera, Tonantzín,
Guadalupe, and farolitos. Knowing these references is crucial to
understanding the full effect and content of the poem. But one can
get a lot from reading the poem without such knowledge. However,
when I find a poem that interests me I feel a need to honor the poet
and learn about the sources of her or his images and metaphors. In
the case of this poem, a Spanish dictionary and a reference guide
to Mexico would be very useful. With the Internet, getting informa-
tion that clarifies the references is quite easy. It also expands one's
own knowledge. Ana Castillo is addressing people who would
know her references, and if some of us don't, we have to make the
effort to be included in her circle of readers.

Finally, here is a poem from Kevin Bowen's *Playing Basketball
with the Viet Cong.* Bowen was a soldier in Vietnam, and his reflec-
tions on the war and on returning to Vietnam years after the fighting
provide elegant and painful meditations on the horrors of being in
the midst of a war, whatever side you happen to find yourself on.
The central image in the poem is stated by the title, "First Casualty."

The important word here is "first." The poem is set in the context of the poet's first experience of the death of one of his fellow soldiers, personalizing it, and using the poem to move us to understand that death in wartime is not casual and that the dying do not disappear from the lives of the living.

First Casualty
They carried him slowly
down the hill.
One hand hung,
grey and freckled.
No one spoke but
stared straight up.
His body, heavy,
rolled back and forth
on the litter.
At LZ Sharon cooks spooned
at last hot food.
One by one the squad
walk back up hill.
"Don't mean nothing,"
someone said.
But all that winter
and into spring
I swear he followed us,
his soul, a surplice
trailing the jungle floor.

5

The Voice
of the Turtle

My beloved spake, and said unto me, Rise up my love, my fair
one, and come away.
For, lo the winter is past, the rain is over and gone;
The flowers appear on the earth; the time of the singing of
birds is come, and the voice of the turtle is heard in our land

When I was in high school a few friends and I began to read
the Old Testament as poetry, with a strong emphasis on the Song
of Solomon, the book of Ruth, and the prophets. It was a respect-
ful way to honor the Bible and at the same time inform our par-
ents that formal religion was not an essential part of our lives. I
loved the image of the voice of the turtle speaking out through the
land. We had pet turtles, some with backs painted with images
from Miami or Coney Island, and I had never heard a sound from
a single turtle. Growing up in the Bronx, I assumed that the
beauty of the voice of the turtle is silence, its escape from the
sounds of the city, its meditative quality. I had no idea of the
sounds of spring, of the sounds of a world devoid of cars and
machines. For years the voice of the turtle was to me the opposite
of song–it was the silences, the pauses that make life tolerable in
a loud world. It was a shock when I learned that the turtle of the
verse was a turtledove, a sweet, seductive sound that called one to
love and flowering.

Since then I have thought of the turtle as a turtledove, and when I see turtles I hear them singing. There was no need to reject the turtle as a songster. It was quite easy, as I became somewhat fluent in poetry as a way of thinking, to make the turtle and the turtledove one.

Poets have the freedom to merge opposites, imagine the unimaginable, break all of the usual rules of language in the service of their sentiments and dreams, and rethink the ordinary ways in which language serves us. It also allows the poet to reaffirm old images of how the world was made and transform them into new sensibilities. In many Native American societies the turtle is so central that the world could not survive without its support. As an example, for the Iroquois the Earth rests on the back of a turtle, he being the only creature that could keep the Earth stable while traveling through the winds and currents of space. The turtle can be benevolent or a trickster, but it is a central image for many Native American peoples.

The poet Gary Snyder titled one of his collections of poems *Turtle Island.* In the introduction to the book he ties the image of Turtle Island to his own poems and to the power of the diverse peoples and voices that make up North America:

> Turtle Island—the old/new name for the continent, based on many creation myths of the people who have been living here for millenia [sic], and reapplied by some of them to "North America" in recent years. Also, an idea found world-wide, of the earth, or cosmos even, sustained by a great turtle or serpent-of-eternity.

> A name: that we may see ourselves more accurately on this continent of watersheds and life-communities—plant zones, physiographic provinces, culture areas; following natural boundaries. The "U.S.A." and its states and counties are arbitrary and inaccurate impositions on what is really here.

The poems speak of place, and the energy-pathways that sustain life. Each living being is a swirl in the flow, a formal turbulence, a "song." The land, the planet itself, is also a living being—at another pace. Anglos, Black people, Chicanos, and others beached up on these shores all share such views at the deepest levels of their old cultural traditions—African, Asian, or European. Hark again to those roots, to see our ancient solidarity, and then to the work of being together on Turtle Island.

Peter Blue Cloud, a poet who is a Turtle Mohawk from Caughnwaga, Quebec, has chosen, in this next poem, to write in a certain voice—not the one he uses at home with his children or with his friends and colleagues, but one that speaks in the voice of the turtle and reflects the Turtle tradition. The poet is not the poem. Rather, the choice of voice for a poem is part of the craft of making poems. This ritual voice of Peter Blue Cloud is only one of many he uses in his poetry. When reading this, as other poems, it's important to be sensitive to the voice the poet chooses and, as a reader, give oneself up to the way in which the poet is presenting the poem to you.

Turtle
The winds are dark passages among the stars,
leading to whirling void pockets
encircled by seeds of thought,
life force of the Creation.
    I am turtle,
and slowly, my great flippers move
propelling my body through space,
and starflowers scatter crystals
which fall as mist upon my lidded eyes.
    I am turtle,
and the ocean of my life swim
is a single chant in the Creation,
as I pass others of my kind,
    my own, unborn, and those,
the holy ancients of my childhood.

My swim is steady and untiring
for great is the burden given me,
the praise and privilege of my eternity
rests upon my back as a single seed
to which I am guardian and giver.
   I am turtle,
and my tribes forever remain countless,
from the day I first raised my head
to gaze back upon the horn of my body,
     and my head was a sun,
     and Creation breathed life upon the seed
     and four times, and again four times,
     I wept for joy the birthing of my tribes,
     and chanted Creation the glory
of all these wondrous days.

The wrinkles and cracks upon this ancient shell
are the natural contours created
by the feel and request of burdened rock
and soil, blood and sustenance to
clans within clans
   I am turtle,
and the earth I carry is but
a particle in the greater Creation,
my mountains, plains and oceans,
mere reflections in a vaster sea.
     Turtle, I am called,
     and breathe clouds of rain,
     and turn slowly my body to seasons
     in cycle with my grandchild, Eagle,
     whose wings enfold thunder pulses.
     back to back, and
seldom meeting in time.

Patience was given me by Creation,
ancient song on tomorrow's wind,
this chant that was taught my tribes
is now unsung by many clans
of a single tribe,
    and truly
such pains that exist for this moment,
which slay so many of the innocent
cannot but end in pain repeated
as all are reflected twins of self.
    I am turtle,
and await the council of my tribes
clan into clan, the merging thought
that evil was never the star path, and
then the chant to the four directions,
    I am turtle,
and death is not yet my robe,
for drums still throb the many
centers of my tribes, and a young
child smiles me of tomorrow,
    "and grandparent,"
another child whispers, "please,
tell again my clan's beginning."

Peter Blue Cloud is not the turtle. The turtle is talking through him. One cannot experience the power of this poem by identifying the turtle with the poet. This is more like religious poetry that is recited in church or temple as part of a sanctified occasion. The repetition of "I am turtle" is reminiscent of the same kinds of repetition one can find in the Koran, the Bible, and in the songs and chants of many traditional religions.

Gary Snyder also chooses a ritual voice for this poem, and reading it is a form of chanting.

> ### Prayer for the Great Family
> Gratitude to Mother Earth, sailing through night and day—
>   and to her soil: rich, rare, and sweet
>   *in our minds so be it.*
> Gratitude to Plants, the sun-facing light-changing leaf
>   and fine root-hairs: standing still through wind
>   and rain: their dance is in the flowing spiral grain
>   *in our minds so be it.*
>
> ## Islands
>   Gratitude to Air, bearing the soaring Swift and the silent
>   Owl at dawn. Breath of our song
>   clear spirit breeze
>   *in our minds so be it.*
>
>   Gratitude to Wild Beings, our brothers, teaching secrets,
>   freedoms, and ways; who share with us their milk;
>   self-complete, brave, and aware
>   *in our minds so be it.*
>
>   Gratitude to Water: clouds, lakes, rivers, glaciers;
>   holding or releasing; streaming through all
>   our bodies salty seas
>   *in our minds so be it.*
>
>   Gratitude to the Sun: blinding pulsing light through
>   trunks of trees, through mists, warming caves where
>   bears and snakes sleep—he who wakes us—
>   *in our minds so be it.*

Gratitude to Great Sky
    who holds billions of stars—and goes yet beyond that—
    beyond all powers, and thoughts
    and yet is within us—
    Grandfather Space.
    The Mind is his Wife.
        so be it.

      after a Mohawk prayer

However, the ritual voice is not the only one Snyder or Blue Cloud use in their poetry. They both have the skill and the complexity to vary their voices according to the content and intent of their poems. Here a second poem by Peter Blue Cloud that has an intimate voice. In "Ochre Iron" his father is at the center of the poem, and Blue Cloud's own personal grief and rage influence his choice of words, line breaks, and images in order to speak with a passion and personal authority. The poem builds to an intensity and anger that encompass feelings not merely about his father's life but about the ways in which the oppression of native peoples has been transmitted from generation to generation. He confronts and tries to expiate the effects of victimization.

This poem will be understood differently by different readers. For Native American readers, it might have resonances and images that allude to experiences they have had. For other oppressed people, it might be a metaphor for their own lives. And for others whose lives have been protected by having the privileges of being members of the sanctioned majority, it can be a metaphor for personal journeys they have undergone or an insight into experiences they have not had. It can also be a challenge to change one's way of thinking. There is no need to speak about the one way to read this poem (and others, of course). It is more a question of understanding how the poet has chosen to sound, what voice has been used, and how you can relate to that voice and that poem.

Ochre Iron
Falling forever
with over and under
falling forever from
pink to purple bridgeways
my father's floating, falling,
decays many schemes
in youth's web-footed anger
    of balance.

I wonder how many, if any,
boyhoods my father portrayed
upon my reservation's
    starving soil,
or how many puppies yapped his heels
as over and over he fell,
or which of the mothers
cast shy eyes at fleeing feet,
    and was it this
same lonesome loon
Falling forever
among wheeling stars
transfixed upon a canvas
    of universes,
my boot's sad dust
in vain retracing
a highway's straight
and naked hostility,
as over and under
    falling forever
I scream his outrage
to echoing hills
and vibrating steel bridges.
    I scream
            falling,
as cities collapse to my cry
and layer upon layer of lies
of twisted iron beams and braces
cut limbs tearing searing pains.

I wonder forever how many
if any, stole of rest within
the rich hayloft world
of another's dreaming,
and how many now deserted
campfires cast a warmth
in a taste of winter
found in hidden springs
    along that lonely highway.
Bent and twisted he sat
fashioning handles of hickory
with eyes always centered within
to stare down the pain,
so young to be an ancient
too tired to want anything,
smiling, at last, crookedly,
when death offered its dark robe.

And grandfather's bones stirred
once in mute grief, and made room
for the son he barely knew
and the pain was passed on
    and on
not only to another son,
but to a tribe.

And falling forever
with over and under,
I clutch at naked sky
to stand on firm earth,
    father,
I live you moment by moment.

At this point it makes sense to reread Robert Bly's poem about his dead father and compare Bly's voice in the poem to that of Peter Blue Cloud. Notice Bly's attention to detail and how he positions himself in this dream experience. Also think of the difference in the tone of the voice, the regret and sadness.

When My Dead Father Called

Last night I dreamt my father called to us.
He was stuck somewhere. It took us
A long time to dress, I don't know why.
The night was snowy; there were long black roads.
Finally, we reached the little town, Bellingham.
There he stood, by a streetlamp in cold wind,
Snow blowing along the sidewalk. I noticed
The uneven sort of shoes that men wore

In the early Forties. And overalls. He was smoking.
Why did it take us so long to get going? Perhaps
He left us somewhere once, or did I simply
Forget he was alone in winter in some town?

Attending to the voices in these two poems is not criticizing them or measuring them against each other. It is more like listening to the ways in which people choose to talk about their experiences and engage the reader and attempt to evoke an authentic response to their work.

Here's yet another poem in which a son encounters his father. In Jaime Jacinto's poem the father is dying and the poem is an expression of anguish, frustration, and love. It's interesting that Jacinto is a Filipino American poet, Bly a European American poet, and Blue Cloud a Native American poet. These different backgrounds shape the language and the context of the poems—but these three poets are all sons and all write about their fathers in ways that are accessible to anyone. The ethnic and the personal often intersect in good poetry in ways that make it universal.

Heaven Is Just Another Country
I'm going to die, he says
not to anyone in particular,
it's the sting of bitterness
he's talking to and at
the head of the table
in a Chinatown restaurant
he orders another scotch
before dinner.
With mother shaking her head,
I help him
from his chair to the john.
He pees slowly
fingers like knobby roots
on his fly, passing a test
of agility for a man this drunk.

I'm dousing cold water on his forehead
and he tells me again he's dying,
Don't say a word to your mother
about this and please forget
you ever saw me this way.

I pretend not to hear,
unaccustomed to the openess
and instead, remember how
you were once a young man
new to America where you learned
to drive a Plymouth sedan
back and forth to work every day,
to sit at a desk chainsmoking
and drawing blueprints for
the houses you never saw.

I want to be seven again
and ride with you on the early morning streets
down Market Street. Across Sixth and Brannan, and beyond
to your desk of scattered papers,
to an ashtray piled with cigarette stubs.

But back home, I watch you slump
into an armchair and sigh
from the whisky that pinches your swollen waist.
Tonight, you say, *heaven is just another*
country and the trip begins
within an airplane like the one you rode
30 years back,
with propellers spinning
so fast you forget
you are in America
inside your living room
and instead,
you are singing at the top of your lungs
like your own son beside you
because far below there is nothing
but blue tide and an ocean crossing.

Voice differs from poet to poet, and also within the work of an individual poet. Being aware of the voice within a poem helps a reader understand the nature of the conversation the poet intends to have with his or her reader. Some poems scream, others seduce. Some let you bear witness to the thoughts and the sentiments of the poet, others invite you to participate, sing, recite. The range and variety of the relationship between poet and reader is large, and thinking about the voice of the poem helps you get ready to read and engage the poet.

It's interesting to read widely in the works of a poet when you discover a poem you admire. As a complex portrait of the poet and her or his voices emerges, you can begin to tease out the common sensibility and linguistic control a poet has from the different voices he or she can use in a poem. The preceding sections of the book contained several of Denise Levertov's poems: "The Secret," "Not to Have," and "Jacob's Ladder." In "The Secret," Levertov talks about some young people who told a friend of hers that they found the secret of life in a line she wrote, but didn't say which line. The voice of the poet is gentle, admiring, and slightly ironic. She shows her love for these young readers in a subtle and yet unashamed way. In "Not to Have" we are taken to the black heart of the poppy. This is an intense, condensed poem that expresses longing and talks about the end of time. Both poems are written with Levertov's sharp ear for the exact right word. There is nothing wasted in her language, no casual conversation with the reader. "Jacob's Ladder" is a biblical exegesis, a metaphysical speculation on the courage of facing the challenges of life and how that provides human life with a dignity and heroic dimension not available to angels. To read Levertov in all her voices is to enter into the most exacting and precise, often philosophical use of language one is likely to encounter. Other poets are deliberately more chatty or go on at greater length. They deal with specific relationships, or tell tales. One way to understand this is to think of the range of music a good singer can perform: blues, ballads, comic songs, political songs, songs that make you dance. The singer has the same voice and is recognizable across all the styles and genres she or he chooses to sing, but the modulation of voice is what makes each work effective and appropriate to the substance of the song.

Levertov's style, in all her voices, is to get to the poetic center of a significant idea, emotion, or event. Here are two more poems by Levertov, one embracing and the other outraged. Read them with a thought to how the poet modulates her voice and at the same time is thoroughly recognizable.

O Taste and See
The world is
not with us enough
O taste and see

the subway Bible poster said,
meaning **the Lord,** meaning
if anything all that lives
to the imagination's tongue,

grief, mercy, language,
tangerine, weather, to
breathe them, bite,
savor, chew, swallow, transform

into our flesh our
deaths, crossing the street, plum, quince,
living in the orchard and being
hungry, and plucking
the fruit

Land of Death-Squads
The vultures thrive,
clustered in lofty blue above
refuse-dumps where humans too
search for food, dreading
what else may be found.
Noble their wingspread,
hideous their descent
to those who know
what they may feast on:
sons, daughters.
And meanwhile,
the quetzal, bird of life, gleaming
green, glittering red, is driven
always further, higher,
into remote ever-dwindling forests.

Here are four poems by Mark Doty that provide wonderful examples of how a poet can modify her or his voice and even take the same theme and idea and speak it differently. The first poem, brief and defiant, begins with a quote from a critic of Doty's poetry.

> **Concerning Some Recent Criticism**
> **of His Work**
> ———*Glaze and shimmer,*
> *luster and gleam;*
>
> *can't he think of anything*
> *but all that sheen?*
>
> ———No such thing,
> the queen said,
> as too many sequins.

Here Doty is angry, pissed off, and getting even. In the next poem, Doty comes back to the criticism, only with a fuller, more personal answer to someone who has criticized his style and, implicitly, his sexual orientation. This second poem goes beyond an answer in kind to a critic, and engages in the question of style, choice, and ways of loving. I find that these two poems reveal the poet at work—starting from a specific response, in this case an insult or a wound, and then moving to a larger canvas and making a statement that anyone who has ever fought to be themselves and no one else's person can understand and find as a source of strength.

> **Concerning Some Recent Criticism**
> **of His Work**
> ———*Glaze and shimmer,*
> *luster and gleam . . .*
>
> ———What else to do
> with what you adore

but build a replica?
My model theater's

an opera of atmospheres:
morning's sun-shot fog

hurried off the stage,
tidal gestures,

twilight's pour:
these gorgeous and
limited elements
which constitute

a universe, or verse.
and if I love

my own coinage,
recombinant elements

(I know, *lacquer*
and *tumble* and *glow,*
burnished and *fired*

and *hazed*) it's because
what else Lord

to wear? Every sequin's
an act of praise.

These bright distillates
mirror the day's

glossed terms——
what's the world but shine

and seem? She'd sewn

the wildly lavish thing
herself, and wore

——forgive me!——shimmer…

Here's a third poem by Doty in a more personal, vulnerable
voice. He is not in attack mode. This poem has an intimate, warm,
funny voice that makes the poet as person come alive. It is a poetic
self-portrait focused on a single moment and a single choice. If
you were to get a tattoo and live with it the rest of your life, what
image would you choose, what part of your body would you deco-
rate, and what would it to do your sense of how you look? These
are the challenges of the poem.

My Tattoo

I thought I wanted to wear
the Sacred Heart, to represent
education through suffering,

how we're pierced to flame.
But when I cruised
the inkshop's dragons,

cobalt tigers and eagles
in billowy smokes
my allegiance wavered.

Butch lexicon,
anchors and arrows,
a sailor's iconic charms——

tempting, but none
of them me. What noun

would you want

spoken on your skin
your whole life through?
I tried to picture what

I'd never want erased
and saw a fire-ring corona
of spiked rays,

flaring tongues
surrounding———an emptiness,
an open space?

I made my mind up.
I sat in the waiting room chair.
then something (my nerve?

faith in the guy
with biker boots
and indigo hands?)

wavered. It wasn't fear;
nothing hurts like grief,
and I'm used to that.

his dreaming needle
was beside the point;
don't I already bear

the etched and flaring marks
of an inky trade?
What once was skin

has turned to something
made: written and revised
beneath these sleeves:

hearts and banners,
daggers and flowers and names.
I fled. Then I came back again;

isn't there always
a little more room
on the skin? It's too late

to be unwritten,
and I'm much too scrawled
to ever be erased.

Go ahead: prick and stipple
and ink me in:
I'll never be naked again.

From here on out,
I wear the sun,
albeit it blue.

And finally, here is the same poet as storyteller. He, and we, are witnesses to a murder, a more effective and upsetting telling than hours of TV thrillers or the cheap killings so common in film these days. This is the death of a person, not just "a death."

Charlie Howard's Descent
Between the bridge and the river
he falls through
a huge portion of night;
it is not as if falling

is something new. Over and over
he slipped into the gulf
between what he knew and how
he was known. What others wanted

open like an abyss: the laughing
stock-clerks at the grocery, women
at the luncheonette amused by his gestures.
What could he do, live

with one hand tied
behind his back? so he began to fall
into the star-faced section
of night between the trestle

and the water because he could not meet
a little town's demands,
and his earrings shone and his wrists
were as limp as they were

I imagine he took the insults in
and made of them a place to live;
we learn to use the names
because they are there,

familiar furniture: faggot
was the bed he slept in, hard
and white, but simple somehow,
queer something sharp
but finally useful, a tool,
all the jokes a chair,
stiff-backed to keep the spine straight,
a table, a lamp. And because

he's fallen for twenty-three years,
despite whatever awkwardness
his flailing arm and legs assume
he is beautiful

and like any good diver
has only an edge of fear
he transforms into grace
Or else he is not afraid,

and in this way climbs back
up the ladder of his fall,
out of the river into the arms
of the three teenage boys

who hurled him from the edge-
really boys now, afraid,
their fathers' cars shivering behind them,
headlights on—and tells them

it's all right, that he knows
they didn't believe him
when he said he couldn't swim,
and blesses his killers

in the way that only the dead

can afford to forgive.

Reading all four of these poems together, a complex picture of a multi-voiced writer emerges. The work is more than the single poem. That is why some of the greatest pleasures of reading poetry derive not from knowing a single poem by a poet, but from being fluent with a body of work, and from listening to their voices as well as reading their words.

6

The Poet's Eye/
The Reader's Eye

Practicing Reading Poetry

> The poet's eye, in a fine frenzy rolling,
> Doth glance from heaven to earth, from earth
>   to heaven;
> And, as imagination bodies forth
> The forms of things unknown, the poet's pen
> Turns them to shapes, and gives to airy nothing
> A local habitation and a name.

It is fitting that this chapter on strategies for reading contemporary poems begins with a quote from Shakespeare. His poetry emerged from performance, and although it is wonderful to read quietly to oneself, it is meant to be played onstage, to be spoken. In addition, the line between contemporary poetry and older poems is not clear—nor are there poets writing now who have not found inspiration and instruction from Shakespeare's work. Across cultural, gender, national, historic, and class boundaries, poetry is a community of the imagination.

> Poetry indeed
>
>   gives to airy nothing
> A local habitation and a name.

Airy nothing is the matter of dreams, perceptions, emotions, and even ideas. The body and the physical world, the specific habitation and name of speculations, insights, celebrations, or sadnesses, are the stuff of poems. Shakespeare is echoed by the first lines of Denise Levertov's "The Secret" (printed in full earlier in the book):

> Two girls discover
> the secret of life
> in a sudden line of
> poetry.
>
> I who don't know the
> secret wrote
> the line.

The secret of life in a line of poetry is that habitation that Shakespeare talks about. It describes the unique way in which a poem can be specific and visceral and at the same time as metaphysical and philosophical. The formal boundaries of academic departments are erased by poetry. A poem does not have to be paraphrased in prose so much as allowed to breathe and sink in. This does not mean that a close analysis of poetry cannot be useful. Rather, it makes sense to analyze a poem after you have learned to read it and come to care for it because it speaks to something deep inside your self. Every poem you read does not have to be analyzed, worked over, or reread. But even poems that have a few lines, images, or phrases that strike you can provide intellectual and spiritual insights.

One way to become intimate with a poem is to take a piece of it that strikes you and recite it out loud in a number of different voices until you feel you have come to voice the poem in a way that allows it to speak to you. I know this sounds romantic and a bit abstract, but think about the voicing of a song. Think of "The Star-Spangled Banner" as sung by Frank Sinatra and as voiced by Jimi Hendrix's guitar. Think of the ways in which "Over the Rainbow" has been sung over the years and has been able to express everything from childhood longing to gay pride. As you learn to voice poems, to speak them out loud and read them silently with the kind of expression, inflection, and feeling that is appropriate not merely to the texts but to your internalization of them, the habit of reading poems can move from the periphery to the center of the activities that provoke you and give you pleasure.

I've found that one way to develop the specific habit of reading poems is to collect short poems or parts of poems that strike me as striking, insightful, or beautiful and copy them into a small notebook. This is my poetry reading notebook: a collection of things I would like to read in my imaginary poetry cafe. These are short poems or fragments of poems, stanzas, lines, phrases that I read, think about, and speak before approaching the complete poem or the whole body of work of a poet I admire. They provide miniatures that I can think about, analyze, and feel my way through.

I've chosen some short poems as well as fragments from longer poems that you've already encountered in this book to suggest ways of developing the habit of reading poetry, thinking about it, and drawing upon it as you try to understand the complexities of being alive in a world that is changing, growing, perhaps spinning out of control or maybe learning how to create a convivial planet. This is a way to revisit poems you've had a chance to encounter before. It's the repetition and practice that internalize the habit of poetry. The reward of doing this is learning new things about old friends. Good poetry continually reveals itself. One does not get a poem once and for all and then leave it behind. Powerful images stay in the imagination and enrich one's thinking and perception. They become part of the memories we can draw upon to understand our experience.

The central issues of our times are unresolved, and the eternal issues such as how to sustain love and relate to the past, the future, and nature are possibly unresolvable. The wonder of poetry is that it does not have to solve the issues or analyze the issues—it can, as Shakespeare expressed it, let the imagination body forth. It is that thrust of the imagination that helps connect people with solutions, with harsh truths, with wicked presumptions—with a sense that everything that you are told in the media, at school, and by the institutions of power is a poor representation of the fullness and uncertainty of the whole of life and experience.

Here are three short poems to read and recite. You've encountered all of them in the book before, and it's worth taking another go at them, this time with the specific intent of performing them—either internally and silently, out loud in the privacy of your home, or among friends and even strangers. Think of this as doing poetry the way you might do music, humming a tune and later listening and discovering the way in which the musicians have transformed that tune into a whole recorded work, and then putting the disk into the CD player and singing along.

The first poem is Charles Simic's "The Road in the Clouds." Skim the poem first, and in your imagination try to be there in bed with the poet.

Your undergarments and mine,
Sent flying around the room
Like a storm of white feathers
Striking the window and ceiling.

Something like repressed laughter
Is in the air
As we lie in sweet content
Drifting off to sleep
With the treetops in purple light

And the sudden memory
Of riding a bicycle
Using no hands
Down a steep winding road
To the blue sea.

This is a love poem, a lovemaking poem, and a poem of daring and adventure, a wild and wonderful event described in language that is restrained, almost puritanical. The word "undergarments" fits with the storm of white feathers that might come from a goose-down coverlet. The sound of them striking the windowpane is not loud or raucous: This is quiet love but deep. There's "repressed laughter," "sweet content," and the marvelous image of riding a bike with no hands. As you read the poem to yourself and as you read it out loud, think of these key words and how to inflect them so that the nuances of this particular kind of lovemaking and the transition to sleep and dreams become a mini-drama. A small picture of how waking falls into sleep and how love can lead to dreams beyond the moment of lovemaking into dreams, memories, and an approximation of the fullness of being.

Here's a second poem, Martin Espada's "The Right Hand of a Mexican Farmworker in Somerset County, Maryland" to reread, perhaps on another day. It does not make sense to read one poem after another the way you try to read through a mystery novel. Poems require thought and concentration, reflection on detail and nuance. They are condensed and, with skilled poets, are full of allusions and connections that emerge on multiple readings. Take time with poems. Here is a poem with a different voice than Simic's, about a thoroughly different subject and with images from another part of human experience:

A rosary tattoo
between thumb
and forefinger
means that
every handful
of crops and dirt
is a prayer,
means that Christ
had hard hands

The habitation and location of the poem in a tattoo immediately grabs the reader. It reveals a deeply felt, permanently imprinted image resting in between those two fingers that make picking a crop possible. When I first encountered this poem I looked at my own hands and could imagine a rosary tattoo, a mark of devotion I would see every time I washed my hands, ate dinner, or did any work. I also remembered my grandfather's hands. There was no tattoo, but the mark of his work was his hands. They felt like the 2x4s that he worked with every day on a construction job. They were not callused, they were *a* callous, as hard and thick as wood. But Pop, as we called him, was a dreamer, an old socialist for whom work had dignity and redemptive value. Even though he was not a Christian, I could see and feel him in the poem and could remember the way in which my grandmother admired my soft hands, which represented to her my escape from the brutality of daily labor as she and her generation knew it.

How to read this poem out loud? Slowly and solemnly? With anger and determination? With reverence, as if it were a prayer or sacred text? Or as a joyful affirmation of the identification of the worker with Christ and by extension with redemption? There is no one way, but as an exercise in getting to the heart of a poem and of contemporary poems, reading this and other poems in as many voices as you can hear in them can be revelatory.

Now try this third, thoroughly different poem by William Carlos Williams, which you've already encountered in the book. In "The Locust Tree in Flower," each line consists of just one word. On first reading try to give every line (that is, every word) equal weight, and then vary the weight of the lines as you feel your way into the sentiment of the poem. Think of reading the poem as if you are reading a musical score for the first time and working your way from the notes of the melody to the inflection and expression of it. I used to play the accordion and remember being given songs to play that I had never heard before. The first time through the melody was simply to get the notes right and be

sure that I heard the whole. It took a while, however, to get from
the notes to the song, and sometimes it takes a while to get from
the words to the poem.

> Among
> of
> green
>
> stiff
> old
> bright
>
> broken
> branch
> come
>
> white
> sweet
> May
>
> again

As an extension of this exercise in reading, here are a number
of fragments from poems already quoted in full in the book. You
might want to look back at the whole poem before investing time
and energy in these short works and fragments.

The first selection I've chosen is from Joy Harjo's "She Had
Some Horses."

> She had some horses.
>
> She had horses who called themselves, "horse."
> She had horses who called themselves, "spirit," and kept
>   their voices secret and to themselves.
> She had horses who had no names.
> She had horses who had books of names.

She had some horses.

She had horses who whispered in the dark, who were
    afraid to speak. She had horses who screamed out
    of fear of the silence, who carried knives to protect
    themselves from ghosts.
She had horses who waited for destruction.
She had horses who waited for resurrection.

She had some horses.

Reading this selection can be quite an adventure. Each line
describes a different kind of "horse" and therefore begs to be read
with a different inflection, tone, and emphasis. Joy Harjo is a
musician as well as a poet, and I can imagine her chanting the
poem. However, it does not need to be sung to be moving and pas-
sionate. After you've tried this selection, you might want to go
back to the whole poem and read it out loud.

The opening lines from Robert Duncan's "After a Long Illness"
pose a different problem for the reader. Look at the spacing, which
really scores the poem for the reader. It is not commas, colons, or peri-
ods that indicate the pauses in the poem, but rather the spacing and
the placement of words on the page. On first reading pay careful atten-
tion to the length of the spacing, the line breaks, the pauses as you
read, and then on a second reading add the emotion that the words
project. It is a poem about being deathly ill and about coming back:

        No faculty not   ill at ease
        let us
        begin where I must

        from the failure of systems   breath
        less,   heart
        and lungs water-logd.

        Clogged with light chains   the kidneys'
        condition is terminal   life

the light and the heavy, the light
and dark.   It has always been
close upon a particular Death, un
disclosed   what's behind

seeing, feeling, tasting, smelling   —that Cloud!

For two years
bitterness pervaded:
in the physical body   the high blood
pressure
     the accumulation of toxins, the
     break-down of ratios,

in the psyche   "stewed in its own juices"

Very different is the ending of June Jordan's "If You Saw a
Negro Lady," in which she reveals that the woman who is the sub-
ject of the poem is celebrating her birthday. How can you read this
revelation? How can the joy and love and poignancy of this moment
be expressed in reading?

If you saw her square
above the dirty
mopped-on antiseptic floors
before the rag-wiped table tops

little finger   broad and stiff
in heavy emulation of a cockney

mannerism

would you turn her treat
into surprise observing
happy birthday

Here are a number of other excerpts from poems quoted in full
throughout the book for you to read and reread. The first is violent,

the second gentle, the third depressed, perhaps melancholy, while the fourth is ironic and a bit zany, and the fifth ritualistic, almost a chant. The sixth excerpt is dreamlike, a bit mysterious, while the final one is reflective. All seven give you a chance to exercise the range of voices poets choose and give you a chance to develop the flexibility and the habit of reading in many voices. It is a way of becoming fluent with the languages of poets.

It's particularly helpful to read the poems out loud. It's fun and it puts you in touch with your own voice as much as with the voices of the poets you read.

1. ⌐ Amiri Baraka *Incident*
   He came back and shot. He shot him. When he came
   back, he shot, and he fell, stumbling, past the
   shadow wood, down, shot, dying, dead, to full halt.

   At the bottom, bleeding, shot dead. He died then, there
   after the fall, the speeding bullet, tore his face
   and blood sprayed fine over the killer and the grey light.

2. ⌐ Li Young-Lee *Blossoms*
   There are days we live
   as if death were nowhere
   in the background, from joy
   to joy to joy, from wing to wing,
   from blossom to blossom to
   impossible blossom, to sweet impossible blossom.

3. ⌐ William Stafford *In Hurricane Canyon*
   How terribly shredded and lonely
   the water went as it cried out and
   held splinters of moonlight, and its
   life raced powerfully on! That night,
   we bowed, shadowed our eyes,
   and followed—all the way down—
   one, slow, helpless, bumping stone.

4. Victor Hernández Cruz *The Problem with Hurricanes*
The campesino takes off his hat—
As a sign of respect
towards the fury of the wind
And says:
Don't worry about the noise
Don't worry about the water
Don't worry about the wind—
If you are going out
beware of mangoes
And all such beautiful
sweet things.

5. Peter Blue Cloud *Turtle*
I am turtle,
and slowly, my great flippers move
propelling my body through space,
and starflowers scatter crystals
which fall as mist upon my lidded eyes.
I am turtle,
and the ocean of my life swim
is a single chant in the Creation,
as I pass others of my kind,
my own, unborn, and those,
the holy ancients of my childhood.

My swim is steady and untiring
for great is the burden given me,
the praise and privilege of my eternity
rests upon my back as a single seed
to which I am guardian and giver.

6. Carolyn Forché *The Recording Angel*
III
The photographs were found at first by mistake in the drawer. After
that I went to
them often

She was standing on her toes in a silk *yukata*, her arms raised
Wearing a girl's white socks and near her feet a vase of calla lilies
Otherwise she wore nothing
And in this one, her long hair is gathered into a white towel
Or tied back not to interfere
She had been wounded by so many men, abused by them
From behind in a silk *yukata*, then like this
One morning they were gone and I searched his belongings for them
like a madwoman
In every direction, melted railyards, felled telegraph poles
For two months to find some trace of her
Footsteps on the floor above. More birds
It might have been less painful had it not been for the photographs
And beyond the paper walls, the red maple
Shirt in the wind of what the past meant
The fresh claw of a swastika on Rue Boulard
A man walking until he can no longer be seen
Don't say I was there. Always say I was never there.

7. ⌐   Mark Doty *My Tattoo*
I thought I wanted to wear
the Sacred Heart, to represent
education through suffering,

how we're pierced to flame.
But when I cruised
the inkshop's dragons,

cobalt tigers and eagles
in billowy smokes
my allegiance wavered.

Butch lexicon,
anchors and arrows,
a sailor's iconic charms——

tempting, but none
of them me. What noun

would you want

spoken on your skin
your whole life through?

After you've played around with these familiar fragments, read
the whole poems keeping in mind the aspects of poetry described
in the book: line breaks and spacing, rhythm and melody, image,
and voice. Here are some questions to ask upon first encountering
the poem, skimming it or reading it through casually for a first time,
and looking at its shape: What do the line breaks look like? How are
the words spaced? How does the poem look on the page? How is the
poet singing his or her song; what is the melody like? How would it
sound if someone else were reading it to you? What images emerge
as central to the poem? And what voice has the poet chosen for this
poem?

As preparation for reading I find it useful to prepare myself by:

1. Reading the first and last lines and stanzas after a preliminary
   first reading. Doing this gives me a sense of the whole and
   helps me navigate through a careful reading of the whole
   poem. I find this particularly useful when reading long poems,
   where it is sometimes easy to get lost in the middle and not
   know where the work is going.

2. Visualizing the central image or metaphor in the fragment so I
   can feel it and see it as well as read the words that describe it.
   It's important to get beyond the words at the same time as appre-
   ciating the sensuous surfaces of the language the poet uses.
   Often the title of the poem provides clues to this image (or of
   multiple images, in the case of some poems), but that's not
   always the case. A first reading will give a greater sense of what
   central governing images or themes the poet addresses in the
   poem. This is a way of approaching the content of a poem
   without trying to paraphrase it in prose. The idea is not to
   reduce a poem to simple declarative sentences, but to keep
   the charisma and openness of the work alive and allow your-

self to be drawn into the work. The idea is not to move away from the poem, but to prepare yourself to be drawn into it.

3. Figuring out a number of tempos or time signatures that might help me read the poem. How fast or slowly do you want to read? What is the range of these different ways of performing the same work? This is a common problem for musicians, and many of them perform the same work at different tempos on different occasion to give the music different readings. It is equally true of actors. Shakespeare is performed so much because the language is brilliant and because there is room for the actor to make that language live in new and different ways with each interpretation of a play and a role. The same is true for poets. If you listen to a poet read his or her poetry a number of times, you find their reading is performance, not recitation. Each time, a different energy, rhythm, and emotion is put into the poem and transforms or puts different emphases on the substance of the work. And as a reader you can and should do the same as you internalize the poem and transform it through your own sensibilities.

4. Examining the line structure of the poem, the breaks and the internal spacing. Remember that poetry uses space in ways that are similar to the way prose uses commas, periods, paragraphs, colons, and semicolons—only poetry is wilder, more flexible, and more visual than prose.

5. Finding a safe space to read, either silently or out loud. I want to relate directly to what I am reading and not to other people's perceptions of me as a reader. I can do that when I choose to share what I love with friends, but a private space for poetry is as important as a private space to practice music, do mathematics, or engage in any creative activity, for that matter.

6. As a final but not necessary suggestion, using a tape recorder and recording my readings. Hearing one's own voice develops the skills of reading poems and provides an indication of the moments in a poem where you don't understand what's being said or, on the other hand, where you really are flowing with the poem and finding a confident and moving marriage between yourself, the poem, and the poet.

7. Copying down a poem, either by hand or on a computer, and reading it to myself as I write it down. I find that copying a poem gives me a greater sense of how it is constructed. It takes me through the work a word and a phrase at a time, and provides a very personal meditation on the poem. It also sets it in my mind and makes reading the poem out loud much easier. Besides, I think it's fun, but I was the kind of kid who liked penmanship in elementary school.

8. Making a personal book of excerpts or lines from poems I like and reading one or more lines every morning. Memorize them. Get your mind going with a tiny bit of poetry before or after breakfast or on the way to work.

9. Memorizing some poems and reciting them whenever I feel like it.

Here are a few poems I believe are worth the investment and time of reading, rereading, and thinking one's way through the text. Instead of my making comments on them, I suggest that you take informal notes on the poems to help you focus on how to read them in ways that move you and might move your friends. Of course, if one or all of them leaves you cold, be honest about that, too, and find another poem in the book or in a bookstore and invest in that work. If it feels comfortable to begin with a form to write down your impressions, here's one that might work:

Poem:
Sketch of Line Structure, Picture of the Poem:

The Rhythm and Melody:
(quote some lines, repetitions, or phrases here)

The Central Image:
(quote from poem as well, using either the title or phrases or lines that set the images that govern the work)

The Voice of the Poet:
(how he or she sounds and words and other aspects of the poem that reveal the voice or voices in the poem)
Here are the poems.

1 ⌐ *Landscape for the Disappeared*
  Yusef Komunyakaa

Lo & behold. Yes, peat bogs
In Louisiana. The dead
stumble home like swamp fog,
our lost uncles & granddaddies
come back to us almost healed.
Knob-fingered & splayfooted,
all the has-been men
& women rise through nighttime
into our slow useless days.

Live oak & cypress
counting these shapes in a dance
human forms aren't made for. Faces
waterlogged into their own
pure expression, unanswerable
questions on their lips.

Dumbstruck premonitions rise
from the heckle-grass
to search us out.
Guilty, sings the screech owl.
I hear the hair keeps growing
in the grave. Here
moss lets down a damp light.

We call back the ones
we've never known, with stories
more ours than theirs.
The wind's low cry
their language, a lunar rainbow
lost among Venus's-flytraps
yellowing in frog spittle & downward mire,
boatloads of contraband
guns & slot machines dumped
through the years.
Here's this lovely face so black

with marsh salt. Her smile,
a place where minnows swim.
All the full presence
shiny as a skull under the skin.
Say it again—we are
spared nothing.

2 ⌐ *Curandera*   (note: a curandera is a traditional healer)
1984
Pat Mora

They think she lives alone
on the edge of town in a two-room house
where she moved when her husband died
at thirty-five of a gunshot wound
in the bed of another woman. The *curandera*
and house have aged together to the rhythm
of the desert.

She wakes early, lights candles before
her sacred statues, brews tea of *yerbabuena*.
She moves down her porch steps, rubs
cool morning sand into her hands, into her arms.
Like a large black bird, she feeds on
the desert, gathering herbs for her basket.

Her days are slow, days of grinding
dried snake into powder, of crushing
wild bees to mix with white wine.
And the townspeople come, hoping
to be touched by her ointments,
her hands, her prayers, her eyes.
She listens to their stories, and she listens
to the desert, always, to the desert.

By sunset she is tired. The wind
strokes the strands of her long gray hair,
the smell of drying plants drifts
into her blood, the sun seeps
into her bones. She dozes
on her back porch. Rocking, rocking.

At night she cooks chopped cactus
and brews more tea. She brushes a layer
of sand from her bed, sand which covers
the table, stove, floor. She blows
the statues clean, the candles out.
Before sleeping, she listens to the message
of the owl and *coyote*. She closes her eyes
and breathes with the mice and snakes
and wind.

3 ⁓ *Love Plumbs to the Center of the Earth*
    Jay Wright

1

I will live with winter
and its sorrows.
Here, the earth folds its blanket
                    at noon.
The eastern crown appears,
disappears,
appears
to lie in pine
on the west ridge.
Some light has been lost;

a stillness has been betrayed.
I seem to feel your body
shake that stillness through the deep
water which separates us now.
Your husband, my father,
plumb of the earth
from our air to his,
lies in the silence of water
we gave to him.

You say you sit at night afraid,
and count the gifts you carried
                    to his bed.
I know that they contain
this fear of the winter's sorrows,
this offense of being left above
the deep water
to pluck this plumb string
of a tremor of love.
But it isn't the melody of loss
you have in your moon bucket,
nor the certainty of a line
                    to your own pain.
The clamor that rides this line
unhinges sorrow,
unburdens its beatific companions.
This single string,
a heart's flow,
is a music of possession.
And so you twin me
in the plain song of survival,
in the deep chant of winter
and its own sun.
Our balance is that body
and the sun extended
                    from our grief.

2

Today,
nine days
after the hunters have gone,
a buck walks from the forest,
and nuzzles at my snow-heavy trees.
I crown him king of the noon,
and watch the light drip from his coat.
In these woods,
his light is a darkness,
an accommodation with winter
and its mid-day shroud.
And, if at night, the moon
holds down its spoon cup,
he will be fed by light
that holds the darkness in it.
His body is the plumb line
the stars shake upon our earth.
Now, will I dare to follow
and to name his steps
through every darkness of our earth,
or shall I turn from that light
to my own winter's light?

3

Left. Right.
Turn. And counterturn.
I would have my foundation stone.
And so I carefully turn my words
about your longing.
Soil, water, root and seed,
the pin of light on which your love
will ride to air finds and turns
in the heart of each of its possessions.
You own me in the grief
                    you will not bear,
and in the act you will not name.

You crown my darkness in your silence,
and you crown me king of my engendered light.
If I possess a seat to rule,
I rule love's coming and the taut
sound of my father's voice in you.
Voices of that deep water stretch
into heaven on a thin line filled
with all we do not possess.

Here are some final suggestions. Listen to poets read their own work on tape and CD. A series of recommendations and suggestions are listed in the appendix. Also, go to poetry readings in your own community. And most fun of all, set up a poetry reading group with some friends and meet for coffee or wine and cheese once or twice a month with the idea of reading poems, talking about them, and perhaps even writing poetry. Over the years I have set up and participated in such groups. Sometimes they have lasted for years, other times for just a few months. The structure of each group is informal and simple. Each person in the room chooses a poem that he or she likes and brings it. During the evening everyone has a chance to read the poem they bring. After each poem is read, it is passed around the room and read out loud by other people so that there are multiple readings and multiple interpretations of each work. Then an informal discussion of the poems takes place, and sometimes people write poems inspired by the poems they read.

Multiple readings are wonderful, as each poem becomes more familiar and confusions are cleared up, sound relationships emerge that are not clear in the first readings, and the images sink in enough. Best of all, reading and understanding poetry becomes a social as well as a personal event.

Appendix:
Reaching Out
and Digging In

Reading More Works of the Poets
Cited in this Book

There are more than fifty poets quoted in this book. Collectively they have written more than three hundred volumes of poetry. I originally thought to recommend a few of those books by including a list of those that I have enjoyed. However, in keeping with what I wish to achieve through this book, I hope that the reader will go out and choose books by the authors that they have enjoyed reading in this book. It also makes sense to read around, look through books in the library and bookstore before settling in to the work of a particular poet. The poets quoted in this book represent only a fraction of the poets I admire and whose work I could easily have chosen to reproduce.

Consequently, instead of recommending specific poems I have made a list of the poets whose work is discussed in this book. I've arranged them alphabetically by first name—Robert Frost instead of Frost, Robert Pinsky instead of Pinsky. I felt it would be friendlier this way, and over the years I have noticed that poets prefer being referred to by their full names rather than simply by their last names.

Using the list you can begin to remember names of writers whose books you might like to skim and eventually might develop the habit of hanging out in the poetry section of the library or in bookstores. This provides an opportunity to discover interesting new work as well as figure out how to dig into the work of poets that already interest you.

Adrienne Rich
Al Young
Allen Ginsberg
Ana Castillo
Carolyn Forché
Charles Simic
Chitra Banerjee Divakaruni
Czeslaw Milosz
David Ignatow
Denise Levertov
Derek Walcott
Gary Snyder
George Oppen
Imamu Amiri Baraka
Jaime Jacinto
Jane Hirshfield
Janice Mirikitani
Jay Wright
John Taggart
Josephine Miles
Joy Harjo
Juan Delgado
June Jordan
Kevin Bowen
Langston Hughes
Li-Young Lee
Marianne Moore
Mark Doty
Mark Strand
Martin Espada
Muriel Rukeyser
Pat Mora
Peter Blue Cloud
Rita Dove
Robert Bly
Robert Creeley

Robert Duncan
Robert Hass
Ron Padgett
Sandra Cisneros
Sherman Alexie
Victor Hernández Cruz
W. D. Snodgrass
William Carlos Williams
William Stafford
Yehuda Amichai
Yusef Komunyakaa

Poetry Anthologies

One way to get a flavor of what is happening in poetry is to read anthologies of contemporary poetry. I do this obsessively, almost always finding some gem or some lines, phrases, and metaphors that illuminate my experience. Most anthologies tie together by central themes such as the ethnicity of the poets, or their gender or sexual orientation. Other anthologies center on political, social, or psychological motifs. Some are tied together simply by the year they were published or by the tastes of the editor. However it, would be a mistake to read the poems in, for example, an anthology of Asian American poets or women poets as if their poems were simply for or about Asian Americans or women. Poetry at its best surpasses all of the categories that are used to package it for publication.

Here is a selection of anthologies that contain poems that I hope will move or interest you. I have kept my comments to a minimum and in many cases the titles and subtitles of the anthologies are self-explanatory and no comment is needed.

Against Forgetting: Twentieth-Century Poetry of Witness, ed. Carolyn
   Forché (W. W. Norton, New York, 1993).
   This is an anthology of poetry of conscience. Here's a quotation by Nelson Mandela about this collection which is one of my favorites:

Poetry cannot block a bullet or still a *sjambok*, but it can bear witness to brutality—thereby cultivating a flower in a graveyard. Carolyn Forché's *Against Forgetting* is itself a blow against tyranny, against prejudice, against injustice. It bears witness to the evil we would prefer to forget but never can—and never should.

Aloud: Voices From Nuyorican Poets Café, ed. Miguel Algarín, Bob Holman (Henry Holt & Company, New York, 1994).
Aloud presents the poetry of people who have been associated with the Nuyorican Poets Cafe on the lower East Side of Manhattan, a must stop for poetry lovers. Much of the poetry comes from the work of Puerto Rican New Yorkers but the range is much wider than that, from founding poets Miguel Piñero, Ntozake Shange, Piri Thomas, to Maggie Estep, Nicole Breedlove, Mike Tyler, Reg E. Gaines, Edwin Torres, Paul Beatty, and Jimmy Santiago Baca.

American Poetry Since 1970: Up Late, selected and introduced by Andrei Codrescu (Four Walls Eight Windows, New York, 1987). This is a wide-ranging anthology that is definitely not oriented toward academic poetry. Codrescu, who does ironic and delightful commentaries on National Public Radio, has made a personal selection of poems that speak in a multiplicity of voices and are accessible and full of energy.

Every Shut Eye Ain't Asleep: An Anthology of Poetry by African Americans Since 1945, ed. Michael Harper and Anthony Walton (Little Brown, New York, 1994).

Harper's Anthology of 20th Century Native American Poetry, ed. Duane Niatum (HarperCollins, New York, 1988).

No More Masks! An Anthology of Twentieth-Century American Women Poets, ed. Florence Howe (HarperCollins, New York, 1993).

Poems for the Millennium: The University of California Book of Modern and Postmodern Poetry Volume II From Post War to Millennium, ed. Jerome Rothenberg and Pierre Joris (University of California Press, Berkeley, California, 1998).
This monumental work of more than seven hundred pages, the second of two volumes on twentieth-century poetry, is worth owning. The poems quoted are from throughout the world and give a much broader sense of the poetry being written throughout the world these days than I have been able present in this book. A treasure, worth investing in.

Poetry Like Bread: Poets of the Political Imagination, ed. Martin Espada (Curbstone Press, Willimantic, Connecticut, 1994).
I agree with Carolyn Forché when she says that:
> This anthology . . . is one of the few collections of poetry that reflects suffering and resistance, as well as the bravery and love that motivate all people who seek a better and more just world. . . . In its political character *Poetry Like Bread* is unique; for the richness of the work it contains, it is essential.

Returning A Borrowed Tongue: An Anthology of Filipino American Poetry, ed. Nick Carbó (Coffee House Press, Minneapolis, Minnesota, 1995).

The Best American Poetry Series, series ed. David Lehman (Scribners Poetry/Simon and Schuster, New York, published annually).
Each volume of this annual series is compiled by a different editor, made even more special because each is also a working poet. For example, in 1997, the volume was edited by James Tate and, in 1996, it was edited by Adrienne Rich. Other editors have included: Richard Howard, Charles Simic, Mark Strand, and Jorie Graham. Naturally the nature of the poetry in each volume is influenced by the taste of the individual editor.

The Open Boat: Poets from Asian America, ed. Garrett Hongo (Doubleday, New York, 1993).

The Rag and Bone Shop of the Heart: Poems for Men, ed. Robert Bly, James Hillman, and Michael Meade (HarperCollins, New York, 1992).

Touching the Fire: Fifteen Poets of Today's Latino Renaissance, ed. Ray González (Anchor Books/Doubleday, New York, 1998).

Books for Digging Deeper: Critical Works on the Nature and Structure of Poetry

There are a number of books that go deeper into the craft of poetry than I have been able to do in this introductory book. If you get hooked on poetry it is definitely worth reading any number of these publications and learning more about poetics. Here are a few books about the craft that I recommend as further steps into the world of poetry:

A Poetry Handbook: A Prose Guide to Understanding and Writing Poetry, Mary Oliver (Harcourt Brace, New York, 1994).
This is a book about the way poems are built. It discusses matters of craft and provides insights into the techniques poets use to condense, shape, and present words, and illuminate experience.

Light Up the Cave, Denise Levertov (New Directions, New York, 1981).
Light Up the Cave contains the full text of the essays excerpted in this book and many more of Denise Levertov's reflections on poetry, politics, and personal life. It is a lovely and sometimes difficult book, but definitely worth reading.

Teachers and Writers Handbook of Poetic Forms, ed. Ron Padgett (Teachers and Writers Collaborative, New York, 1987).
This delightful compendium defines seventy-four basic poetic forms, sketches their histories, and provides examples. The

book also provides a gentle and helping voice on how to read different poetic forms.

The Life of Poetry, Muriel Rukeyser (Paris Press, Ashfield, Massachusetts, 1996).

Alice Walker said of this book and its author:

> Muriel Rukeyser loved poetry more than anyone I've ever known. She also believed it could change the world, move the world. This deep and challenging book is testament to her faith that we need not encounter poetry with fear. That openness to poetry opens us to our most essential inner life.

The Oxford Companion to Twentieth Century Poetry, ed. Ian Hamilton (Oxford University Press, New York, 1993).

This is not a collection of poems, nor does it say much about the nature of poetry. However, it does provide biographies of contemporary poets, including poets whose work you have encountered in this book. It fills in details, brings each poet to life by offering personal insight and providing an overview of each poet's complete works and influences. I love to peruse it, and find that it is a great gift for poetry lovers.

The Poet and the Poem, Judson Jerome (Writers Digest, Cincinnati, Ohio, 1974).

This is an idiosyncratic, delightful book on the magic and the craft of poetry. It is full of interesting examples and ranges across both genre and history. I have found it very useful because the author's love of poetry and desire to communicate about it are palpable and infectious.

The Sounds of Poetry: A Brief Guide, Robert Pinsky (Farrar, Straus, and Giroux, New York, 1998).

This book by Poet Laureate Robert Pinsky discusses poetry as a vocal art. I have not encountered a better book on the sounds of poetry; on reading and singing poems, and feeling them in your body.

Poets on Poetry

Finally, here are three books in which poets talk about their own poems as well as other poems that they admire. These books provide insight into how poets think and work. As a reader of poetry I find they are especially useful in helping to understand the experiments poets make with words; the approximations they make before they feel they have the language and sound right and the spirit of the poem coherent.

Ecstatic Occasions, Expedient Forms: 85 Leading Contemporary Poets Select and Comment on Their Poems, ed. David Lehman (University of Michigan Press, Ann Arbor, Michigan, 1996).

Poetspeak: In their Work and About Their Work, ed. Paul B. Janeczko (Collier Books, New York, 1991).

What Will Suffice: Contemporary American Poets on the Art of Poetry, ed. Christopher Buckley and Christopher Merrill (Gibbs-Smith Publisher, Salt Lake City, Utah, 1995).

Permissions

Sherman Alexie, "The Exaggeration of Despair," Reprinted from *The Summer of Black Widow*, Copyright © 1996 by Sherman Alexie, by permission of Hanging Loose Press..

Yehuda Amichai, "A Pity. We Were Such a Good Invention," *Love Poems*, Harper and Row, New York, 1981.

Amiri Baraka, "Incident," from *Black Magic: Sabotage, Target Study, Black Art, Collected Poetry 1961–1967*. Reprinted by permission of Sterling Lord Literistic, Inc. Copyright © 1969 by Amiri Baraka.

Robert Bly, "When My Dead Father Called," from *Morning Poems*, HarperCollins Publishers, New York, 1997.

Kevin Bowen, "First Casualty," from *Playing Basketball With The Viet Cong*, 1994. Reprinted with permission of Curbstone Press. Distributed by Consortium.

Ana Castillo, "You Are Real as Earth, y Más," from *Floricanto Sí! A Collection of Latina Poetry*, Penguin Books, New York, 1998. This poem originally appeared in *Berkeley Poetry Review, No. 25*, 1991–1992.

Robert Creeley, "I Know a Man," from *Selected Poems*, Reprinted with permission of University of California Press, Berkeley, CA, 1991.

Victor Hernándex Cruz, "The Man Who Came to the Last Floor," from *Mainland*, Random House, New York, 1973. Copyright © 1973 Victor Hernández Cruz. "Problems with Hurricanes," from *Red*

Muriel Rukeyser, "Islands," from *The Gates*, McGraw Hill, New York, 1976.

Charles Simic, "Slaughterhouse Flies" and "The Road in the Clouds," from *Walking the Black Cat*, Harcourt Brace & Co., New York, 1966.

W. D. Snodgrass, "Owls," *Poetspeak*, A Selection by Paul B. Janeczko, Collier Books, 1991.

Gary Snyder, "Introductory Note" and "Prayer for the Great Family," from *Turtle Island*, New Directions Publishing Co., New York, 1974. Reprinted by permission of New Directions Publishing Co.

William Stafford, "In Hurricane Canyon" and "Why I Am a Poet," from *My Name Is William Tell*, Confluence Press, Lewiston, MD, 1992. Copyright © 1992 by William Stafford. Reprinted by the permission of Confluence Press.

John Taggart, "Monk" from *Loop*, Sun and Moon Press, Los Angeles, CA, 1991.

Derek Walcott, "X," from *Midsummer* in *Collected Poems 1948–1984*. Reprinted by permission of Farrar, Straus & Giroux, Inc., New York, 1986.

William Carlos Williams, "The Red Wheelbarrow," "The Attic Which Is Desire," and "The Locust Tree in Flower," from *The Collected Works of William Carlos Williams, Vol. I and II*, New Directions Publishing Co., New York, 1986, 1988. Reprinted by permission of New Directions Publishing Co.

Jay Wright, "Love Plumbs to the Center of the Earth," from *Explications/Interpretations*, Callaloo Poetry Series, University of Kentucky Press. Copyright © 1984 by Jay Wright.

Al Young, "A Song for Little Children," from *The Song Turning Back on Itself*, Henry Holt & Company, Inc., New York, 1971. Reprinted by permission of the author.